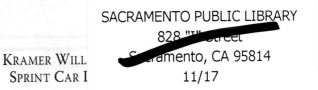
KRAMER WILL
SPRINT CAR I

ID0761269

Kramer Williamson, Sprint Car Legend

Chad Wayne Culver

Foreword by Ken Schrader

McFarland & Company, Inc., Publishers

Jefferson, North Carolina

All photographs courtesy the Williamson family.

Library of Congress Cataloguing-in-Publication Data

Names: Culver, Chad, author.
Title: Kramer Williamson, Sprint car legend / Chad Wayne Culver ; foreword by Ken Schrader.
Description: Jefferson, North Carolina : McFarland & Company, Inc., Publishers, 2017 | Includes bibliographical references and index.
Identifiers: LCCN 2017028614 | ISBN 9781476666976 (softcover : acid free paper) ∞
Subjects: LCSH: Williamson, Kramer Earl, 1950–2013. | Automobile racing—United States—Biography. | Sprint cars—United States—History.
Classification: LCC GV1032.C83 A3 2017 | DDC 796.72092 [B]—dc23
LC record available at https://lccn.loc.gov/2017028614

British Library cataloguing data are available

ISBN (print) 978-1-4766-6697-6
ISBN (ebook) 978-1-4766-2857-8

Front cover: Kramer Williamson and his No. 73 "Pink Panther" Sprint Car in his first appearance at Reading Fairgrounds Speedway on March 12, 1972 (courtesy the Williamson family).

Printed in the United States of America

McFarland & Company, Inc., Publishers
Box 611, Jefferson, North Carolina 28640
www.mcfarlandpub.com

Acknowledgments

I would like to express my sincerest gratitude to all those who helped me tell the story of Sprint Car legend Kramer Williamson. First and foremost, a big thank you to Sharon and Felecia Williamson for working with me on this mammoth undertaking, for being so hospitable, and for welcoming me into their world with open arms. It was an honor to write this book about Kramer and I hope it is a fitting tribute. Thanks to my editor in chief—my wife April—whom I could not do without; April spent countless hours reading over pages and her constant encouragement was always near. Many thanks also to my daughter Ava for her encouragement and her always interesting seven-year-old perspective, and to my mom and dad for their support in everything I do. To my many friends involved in racing in one form or another from the mid–Atlantic area: Your conversations, enthusiasm and knowledge never cease to amaze me. There are too many people to list here, but you know who you are and your friendships are greatly appreciated.

There are so many others I interviewed who added valuable perspective and great stories about Kramer to this book. A big thanks goes to the following: Kurtis Williamson, Lynn Paxton and the staff at the Eastern Museum of Motor Racing, Doug Wolfgang, George Williamson, Davey Brown, Sr., John Zimmerman, Greg Coverdale, Tim Hogue, Al Hamilton, Tim Hamilton, Dale Hammaker, Alan Kreitzer, Charlie Cathel, Chris Gustin, Cliff Irvin, and all the race fans who have encouraged me in the completion of this project.

Table of Contents

Foreword
by Ken Schrader

Even though our racing careers crossed paths only a handful of times, I have been told that Kramer Williamson and I were a lot alike. Maybe not in driving styles, but in temperament and our approach to racing. Kramer enjoyed racing and saw it as fun—I still do. Kramer's family supported his racing and my family has always supported me. His parents played a pivotal role in his career, as did mine. Kramer started racing early in his life, as I did. Being a professional race car driver has been as fulfilling a career for me as I am guessing it was for Kramer.

Throughout Kramer's career he competed among several sanctioning bodies and drove different types of cars, while excelling in Sprint Cars. His career took him many places in the United States, Canada and even Australia. His nickname, "The Pink Panther," is well known among racers and fans. Painting his cars pink was definitely a conversation starter, which led to much ribbing, and some long-lasting relationships throughout Kramer's life. Early in his career, the Williamson family voted on pink as the color of Kramer's race cars, primarily because that was the color of his Mustang. Many men wouldn't buy Kramer's T-shirts because of the color—now everyone has pink shirts and race cars! Drivers, race fans and even those attending a race for the first time will always remember "The Pink Panther"! I give him credit for taking on the teasing and becoming so memorable for his on-track stats, and also for being a bit ahead of his time with the color choice!

Many racers get married and have families. Many of us, myself included, planned our weddings around the racing schedule. Kramer and Sharon Williamson were married at 11 a.m. on August 14, 1976, had the reception, and headed for Selinsgrove Speedway. After he paid for

1

pit passes, the race was rained out. Following a nice dinner with friends, Kramer and his bride headed to a motel—where Kramer discovered he didn't have enough money for the room, yet somehow convinced the clerk to give it to them anyway! That's my kind of family—Ann and I got married at noon on a Tuesday and our honeymoon was basically spent at the race track!

As you read this book, keep in mind the following about Kramer: he was a champion, both on and off the track; he raced for more than four decades; he built and maintained his own equipment; he was a National Sprint Car Hall of Fame inductee in 2008; and he was a family man. All of this, along with his phenomenal racing statistics, made him a true legend of the American motor sports community. Being inducted into the National Sprint Car Hall of Fame is a big deal! And to Kramer, it was a *really* big deal. So much, in fact, that he drove his toterhome sixteen straight hours to get to Knoxville, Iowa. Everyone else on the trip was hungry and grouchy upon arrival, but it was a memorable family trip and Kramer was in his glory as he accepted his Hall of Fame award! As a racer, I can relate to many hours behind the wheel of a truck to get to a race track, a dinner, a sponsor event—it is a part of who we are as race car drivers.

From everything I know and have been told about Kramer, I truly believe that he would have wanted to race right up until the end—just as he did.

Many books have been written about race car drivers, crew chiefs, car owners and visionaries within our sport. Author Chad Culver does an excellent job in exploring and explaining Kramer's career while drawing the reader in to reminisce about and enjoy this much-loved legend of our sport. From the green flag until the checkered flag, you will be an insider, sharing in this truly talented racer's life.

Ken Schrader has successfully raced a variety of race cars on both dirt and asphalt. Schrader is the 1982 USAC Silver Crown Series Champion and the 1983 USAC Sprint Car Series Champion. He has 18 wins in the ARCA Series and has also won races in all three of NASCAR's premier series: the NASCAR Camping World Truck Series, NASCAR Xfinity Series, and the NASCAR Sprint Cup Series. A racer's racer, Schrader continues to race on both dirt and asphalt as many as 100 times a year.

Preface

I can still remember the first time I watched Kramer Williamson race when I was a child. Growing up in the shadow of US 13 Dragway & Speedway (Delaware International Speedway) in Delmar, Delaware, I attended the races with my dad every Saturday night. It was always a special treat when the URC (United Racing Company) Sprint Cars came into town and put on a show. No other car looked like Kramer's and no one else drove like Kramer. When the bright #73 "Pink Panther" Sprint Car pulled out onto the track, you could not miss it and you knew you were in for a show.

When I was growing up, my heroes were always race car drivers. I watched drivers like Richard Petty and Bobby Allison at Dover Downs Speedway and on TV, but nothing compared to the absolute awe of watching an expert driver navigate around a dirt oval in a fire-breathing Sprint Car. Kramer, as he was simply known to his fans, caught my eye right away. His pink car the easiest to spot and, once you watched him pilot it around the track for a few laps, you knew you were watching an artist paint his canvas. Kramer's smooth but aggressive driving style made me an instant fan.

As years rolled by and I grew older, my dad let me venture into the pits to get up close with the cars and drivers. I would check in on my regular heroes every week in the Modified and Late Model division, but when the Sprint Cars were in town, there was just one guy I wanted to see: Kramer. I guess I was expecting to meet a cocky, brash driver who had a big ego and no time to talk, but that was not who I met at all. Instead, I met a man who was generous, warm and willing to take time from prepping his car for the night's race to show a kid around the cockpit of a race car. This was Kramer Williamson. Looking and acting more like the uncle in your family who everyone loved to hang around with, he was a racer's racer. Kramer treated every fan like family—and he had lots of fans.

Throughout the years, Kramer had great success at the one-half-mile dirt oval known as US 13. It was only later, when I became interested in racing history, that I realized just how legendary his career was. In the Sprint Car mecca known as Pennsylvania, Kramer was a living legend. Home to some of the best Sprint Car racers in the world, Pennsylvania also has some of the most unusual, toughest tracks in the country. (Just ask some of the World of Outlaws drivers how hard it is to win in a race in Pennsylvania.) Kramer beat the best in the world on a regular basis, winning championships along the way. In a career that spanned from 1968 to 2013, he earned legions of fans, most of which were clearly visible in the grandstands wearing T-shirts bearing images of their hero in his trademark color pink.

I was there when Kramer won his last race at US 13 on April 30, 2011. I have to say, watching that pink Sprint Car pull into Victory Lane made me feel like a kid again and brought back many good memories of my time at the track as a child. I was amazed that after forty-five years of racing and at sixty years old, Kramer could still get it done on the track. I can't remember a more popular Sprint Car victory at US 13 ever.

I was sitting in the same spot a little over two years later in 2013 watching a Modified qualifier when a friend came up to my seat and told us that he had just heard Kramer had a bad wreck at Lincoln Speedway in Pennsylvania. Word travels fast in the racing community and we all hoped and prayed for the best that night. Sadly, Kramer Williamson succumbed to his injuries the next day, August 4, 2013.

Kramer Williamson, Sprint Car Legend covers his racing career from his humble beginnings racing karts in 1968 to his epic Hall of Fame Sprint Car career and beyond. By interviewing competitors, owners, friends and family—those who knew Kramer best—we will ride along with his incredible journey through life and find out what made Kramer a racing legend. The statistics and wins only tell part of the story. The impact Kramer had on his fans, friends, competitors and family will live on forever.

Introduction

As my car crosses the running waters of the Susquehanna River and passes numerous large barns weathered from their years of service, I can hear a train whistle from miles away and am taken back to simpler times. These sights and sounds are all signs of just how special this area is. Upon pulling up to a stoplight, I spot a Sprint Car parked across the road from my car at a local gas station and am reminded that this is Sprint Car country. This is central Pennsylvania. The same scene is played out throughout the many small towns that make up arguably one of the best, most competitive centers for racing in America. Legendary tracks with long racing histories, such as Williams Grove Speedway, Lincoln Speedway, and Selinsgrove Speedway, as well as many others, are all located nearby. With such racing history comes some of the best racers in the nation as well as some of the most rabid, loyal and informed race fans in the world.

My destination is Palmyra, Pennsylvania, a small town located next to the world's center for all things chocolate—Hershey. Palmyra is like many small, blue-collar towns in America. Modest well-kept houses with neatly manicured lawns line the streets. It is spring and the students at the local school are outside having a field day as I reach my destination. Although this house is located on an unassuming, quiet side street, it is not like the others. The simple white home greets me with a hot pink #73 on the garage door. I know that I have found the right place. This is the home of Sprint Car legend Kramer Williamson.

One notices immediately upon entering the first floor that this was the home of a true racer. Kramer Williamson lived, ate and breathed racing his entire life and his home is true evidence of that. The first floor of the home is a race shop, with living quarters on the second floor. The race shop consists of everything one would need to build, maintain and race a Sprint Car. Parts line every wall in the shop. Lathes, tubing benders and other fabrication machinery are located in the far corner. Frame tables lie scattered around the shop as if they are waiting for the next car to be built. Racks of tools and well-organized trays of nuts and bolts remain frozen in time waiting for Kramer to build his next masterpiece. In the back sits something that any fan of Sprint Car racing would easily recognize: the bright pink #73 race car that Kramer made so famous throughout his racing career. Behind the car are trophies, hundreds of trophies. Evidence of a long and storied career that spanned over forty years.

The walls of the upstairs living area are covered with photos of victories, like Kramer's 1978 National Open win at Williams Grove Speedway; championships won, including his three United Racing Club Championships; and family moments, like his induction into the National Sprint Car Hall of Fame. One realizes right away that this was a family affair. In almost every photo are four figures—Kramer, his wife Sharon, their son Kurtis, and their daughter Felecia. Awards and trophies of over 40 years of racing memories lie neatly arranged in almost every room of the home. In the corner of the living room stands a large, aged trophy from the 1978 National Open at Williams Grove Speedway. The fact that it is kept in the house and not in the garage gives a hint to its importance. Scrapbook upon scrapbook line the coffee table, all meticulously preserved and maintained by Kramer's loving wife Sharon, and showcasing his Hall of Fame career. Years of memories preserved, celebrating one of the greatest Sprint Car drivers in the sport's history.

Kramer Williamson was a racer's racer and lived life his way and on his terms. From his humble beginnings racing a Super Sportsman car at Silver Spring Speedway in 1968 until his tragic passing on August 4, 2013, Kramer left a racing legacy that would become legendary throughout the country and around the world. Former United Racing Club President John Zimmerman remembers Kramer's star power well: "You could go to any Sprint Car track in the United States and say the name Kramer and everyone there would know who that was. He knew all the Outlaws and knew Jeff Gordon and Tony Stewart. There are only three to five other race car drivers that would have that same effect. He was a legend in our sport." Although Kramer was a giant in the close-knit Sprint Car racing community, his story is unknown to many, and his humble beginnings would lead to greatness that only a few came to know.

1

Humble Beginnings

George Earl Williamson, Sr., and wife Alfreda Williamson welcomed their firstborn son, Kramer Earl Williamson, on June 26, 1950, in Columbus, Ohio. Kramer's dad, who went by Earl, was employed by the railroad, and like many railroad workers, would pack up the family and move every time a promotion was available. Three different times the Williamsons moved to Pennsylvania so he could work at a place called Genoli Yards. Younger brother George Williamson, Jr., would be born in Indianapolis, and both he and Kramer would attend many schools throughout their young lives. Pittsburgh, Chicago, and other railroad towns scattered around the central and eastern parts of the United States would be visited as well. Born to a blue-collar hardworking family with constant moving and middle-of-the-night calls surely instilled a strong work ethic in Kramer at a young age.

Kramer's early love of racing can most likely be traced to his father. Earl Williamson raced flat-track motorcycles in southern Ohio. While Earl loved to race, he was not so sure his mother would share the same sentiment so he would sneak off to the tracks and race under the assumed name Bill Georgeson. Many racers have used aliases over the years to disguise their real identity to those in the stands as well as any results that the local papers may publish. As Earl progressed in his motorcycle racing, he started to have some success and began to win many races at tracks in the area. Thinking he had put one over on his mother, Earl sat down one Sunday morning for breakfast after a night of racing. His mother, reading the local paper, said casually, "Hey! This Bill Georgeson must be quite a motorcycle racer. I see he is winning a bunch of races." Earl instantly knew he had been found out and his mother knew all about his racing exploits. Earl's racing career came to an end when he suffered a compound fracture to his leg in a motorcycle accident on the street and not in a racing event. Though he could not race competitively anymore, his love of racing never wavered and he remained close to the sport he loved.

Being an executive in the railroad business kept Earl busy providing for his family and unable to venture into any kind of auto racing for himself. A young Kramer would often emulate his father's antics on a motorcycle, and at the age of twelve he strapped a motor to his bicycle, showcasing his mechanical ability that he would become well known for later in his racing career. As the family settled down in central Pennsylvania, Earl did find time to go Kart racing with sons. The Williamsons' Chevy Corvair would tow their double-decker trailer holding two Karts to the track in style, and it was not long before Kramer won several Karting championships. Kramer's younger brother George Jr. remembers to this day his older brother's racing talent.

> Kramer was in all my paths one of the most talented drivers I ever witnessed. Nobody I have ever seen was more naturally talented in anything they did. His very first Sprint Car race he ever ran at Susquehanna in 1971

Kramer (right) and his father Earl (left) pose for a photograph next to the family's Corvair and unique double-decker Kart trailer.

he finished 11th, the next race he ran he finished 8th, the next race he finished 4th and the fourth race he ever ran he won! You just don't hear stuff like that.

Before climbing into a Sprint Car, though, Kramer would have to cut his teeth in the tough Super Sportsman Class at Silver Spring Speedway just outside of Mechanicsburg, Pennsylvania.

Nearing his 18th birthday and still attending high school, Kramer convinced his father to sell both his and his brother's Karts and purchase a Super Sportsman car. Rules at the time dictated that drivers must be 18 years of age to compete at the three-eighths-mile ultra-competitive dirt oval called Silver Spring Speedway. A used Super Sportsman car was purchased from Bob Highland for Kramer to race after he turned 18. As June of 1968 approached, the Williamson family got to work preparing the car for Kramer's rookie season.

Kramer's most recognizable trademark was probably driving a bright pink race car for most of his racing career. The story of how that came to be was from his rookie season, and like most things with the Williamsons, it was a family decision. Younger brother George Jr. remembers exactly how Kramer's car came to be painted the famous pink hue:

Back while Kramer was in high school, a guy named John Mackison who was an amazing, brilliant driver in his time ran the number 1080 on his race car with Davey Brown as the mechanic. He was the sales manager for a Ford dealership in York, Pennsylvania, and Kramer had saved up some money by working at the local gas station to buy a car. When asked by Kramer's dad what kind of car he wanted, Kramer said a Ford Mustang. Kramer was told to look around and see what he could find and if he found a used Mustang to bring it by and his dad would take a look at it. The very first car he brought by the house was a 1966 black and gold Ford Shelby Mustang. Kramer pulled in the driveway with the car salesman to show Dad the car. Dad walked around the car and said this car seems kind of nice. After firing it up and driving less than a mile down the road, Dad said, No, no, no, turn this thing around and go back to the house. Dad said, no way! No way! Not that car. So Kramer was very upset, obviously. So Dad called John Mackison to see if they had any Mustangs on the lot and that his son would like to buy a Mustang. Mackison said they did and that they had a 1967 leftover model and he would give him a heck of a deal on it for $2750. Earl said that sounded great and the family would be right down to look at it. So the whole family gets in the car and rides down to the Ford dealership to see this car. When we all got there and look out in the parking lot and John walks us out to this pink Mustang. I believe the color's name was "Dusty Rose." Kramer's initial reaction was no! no! no! There was no way he was interested in that. Of course Dad, being a tough cookie, said it's this car or nothing, right now, what's it going to be? Kramer was so upset over the color of the Mustang that he was almost crying. He immediately got in his mind he was going to take this Mustang home and he was going to paint it blue, which was the color he originally wanted. So for $2750, Kramer rolled home with his first car, a 1967 pink Mustang. Immediately upon driving the car to school, all the girls in the whole school went nuts over his car. So from the verge of disaster of buying a pink car, all of a sudden, Kramer was a very cool guy in school. Before long, a set of mag wheels went on it as well as shackles to jack up the rear of the car. This was in 1968, around the same time we purchased the race car from Highland that year. Kramer was not allowed to drive the race car until he turned 18. The color of the Mustang became so popular with people that the family decided to paint the race car the same color as the Mustang and that's where the color came from.

Although Kramer ran many different numbers throughout his racing career for many other car owners, when running his own car Kramer always ran #73. The number came from a racing hero of Kramer's named Len "Mugs" Maguire. Mugs was a union electrician for PP&L who ran in both the Hobby Stock division and Super Sportsman. Mugs

Kramer dives to the inside during his rookie year of racing. Throughout his career, Kramer would become famous for his ability to run the bottom of the track.

had limited success in both classes, but Kramer would go down and visit him often in his race shop. Mugs ran the #72 on his race cars, and back in the day you were not allowed to duplicate numbers, so Kramer just chose the next one: 73 would be the number he would most be associated with for his career. In his own words, Kramer shared his feeling about Mugs and the #73: "When I first started, a man named Mugs Maguire had a number 72. So I said I wanted to be one better than him, so I went to 73. He was a real fine individual. He would give you the shirt off his back." Sadly, Kramer's hero, Mugs, was killed in an electrical accident early in Kramer's career, but the impression he left on Kramer lasted for the rest of his life.

During the summer break between his junior and senior years at Cumberland Valley High School and after his 18th birthday in June, Kramer would compete in his first Sportsman car race in July of 1968. Although Kramer would get a late start in the racing season that year, his natural ability and talent behind the wheel of a race car were immediately evident. While he only competed for two months, his results impressed many, and it was enough to earn the coveted Rookie of the Year title at Silver Springs Raceway.

Kramer's early success on the track in 1968 led to the family's going all in for the 1969 race season. Over the following winter, Kramer and his ever-supportive family would purchase a Dick Tobias chassis for the 1969 race season at Silver Spring. With a new car kept in shape by John Frey and support from his whole family, the 18-year-old high school senior was about to jump straight into one of the most competitive scenes in all of racing. Kramer's natural talent and smooth driving style would lead him to four feature wins during the 1969 race season. Even more unbelievable than the four wins was the fact that at 18 years of age, Kramer Williamson would win the 1969 Silver Spring Speedway Sportsman Championship. Lincoln Speedway promoter Alan Kreitzer remembers the impact Kramer had during his early career at Silver Spring Speedway:

> Kramer won the Championship at Silver Springs in 1969 during his second year in racing and being only a senior in high school. I can't begin to tell you what an accomplishment that was. Silver Spring at that time would get forty to fifty cars per night and there were guys who had raced there for twenty years. All of a sudden here comes this kid, this eighteen-year-old kid still in high school beating these old guys. It was really quite something. At that time, Silver Spring was more like local than regional. So it was almost

Kramer (center) in Victory Lane at Silver Spring Speedway during one of his four victories in his 1969 championship year (by Fred Smith).

like in college football where you have West Virginia playing Pittsburgh or something where you have a real hometown rivalry and that's how Silver Spring was because everybody knew everybody. It was a small sphere of people. So for Kramer to come in here and beat those guys, he was quite the polarizing figure. People either loved him or hated him because he was the champion and he was the Dale Earnhardt–type guy where he created a lot of excitement both ways. Kramer had a good team and supportive family. I remember his dad, Earl, his mom Alfreda, his grandma Ditty, all who came to the races every week, and George, his younger brother, who was already into lettering race cars at a very young age.

His style and maturity at the young age of eighteen also had much to do with his success. When asked about his driving style in those early days, Alan Kreitzer says:

He was a go-karter and he was just always smooth. He was never a wild Mitch Smith–type driver. He was always under control and always looking for the fastest way around the track. Even at a young age at Silver Spring, he was smooth and did not crash, which was unusual for such a young guy. He never crashed much his entire career. Silver Springs rewarded that type of smoothness because it was small and tight and you had to capitalize on someone else's mistakes and he was there to take advantage of that. The other thing that made Kramer so successful throughout his career was that he was not just a "black bagger." By that, I mean he was not just a guy that carried his helmet to the race track and got in a car. He was technical in his approach to racing. Even after he stopped racing at Silver Spring and moved on, his cars were the dominant cars at Silver Spring. The Kramer Kraft cars led the field. It was his technical prowess that made him really good. He not only knew how to drive the car, but he knew how to how adjust the car to make it work.

Kramer learned quickly that while many loved this new young champion, not everyone liked the new kid on the block coming in and beating their local heroes. Although Kramer earned the Most Popular Driver Award in 1969 at Silver Spring, some drivers and fans took issue with a high school student coming in and winning a championship. Many fans and drivers would throw pink pacifiers and rattles at the car while it was in the pits. Kramer's biggest fan, his mom, would save these mementos from his early racing days and pass them on to his future wife,

A young Kramer Williamson prepares for the night's events at Silver Spring Speedway behind the wheel of his family owned #73 Sportsman car.

Sharon. In the Williamson house today, a table in the corner of the living room holds these items on display, a reminder of humble beginnings and the fact that not everyone likes a winner.

Throughout all the name-calling, having baby toys thrown at him, and the steep learning curve of driving a dirt race car, Kramer persevered and wore the title of Silver Spring Speedway Super Sportsman Champion with pride. His statistics for that year remain impressive. In 25 races in his sophomore year, he finished in the top five nineteen times, winning four times, with one of the wins being the big Memorial Day 35-lap feature. The new high school graduate had much going for him in 1969 and the future certainly was looking bright. Upon his completion of high school, Kramer would go on to attend Williamsport Area Community College and major in auto mechanics. While Kramer avoided the much-dreaded sophomore jinx in his second year of racing, his third year of racing would see much frustration and a change in his focus. This change would lead him directly to Sprint Cars.

The 1970 season would be a pivotal year in which Kramer continued his winning ways in the #73 Sportsman car, but frustrations and an incident mid-year at Silver Spring raceway would keep him from racing until early 1971. Kramer and his family wisely used that time to set focus on what would be the next chapter in his racing career. Kramer started the 1970 racing season back at Silver Spring raceway in defense of his track championship. He picked up right where he had left off in the 1969 season, and by mid-year Kramer found himself leading the points and making a run for what could possibly be a second and back-to-back championship. Kramer's younger brother George Jr. remembers the situation in 1970 well:

> They were picking on Kramer something terrible and then one night while he was leading in points in 1970 halfway through the season, there was a wreck on the first lap. Back then, the Sportsman cars had transmission clutches, so Kramer stopped and backed up, then drove around the wreck and had to go in through a little bit of the infield to continue, and even the cars that went into the pits to get repaired and everything were allowed to start in front of Kramer. They made him start dead last. Dad was livid! He came right out onto the track and motioned for Kramer to come in and that was it, they sold the car the next week and never went back again.

In a 1974 Area Auto Racing News (AARN) article, the then twenty-three-year-old Kramer reflected fondly on his days racing Super Sportsman cars.

I still talk about the time we were running Sportsman. We went up near New York State. We'd never seen the track before [Penn-Can Speedway] and we won a hundred-lapper. We found out later that we had the smallest engine there, a 302 cubic inch motor. The guy that finished second had a 327, and the guy that finished third had a 350. That had to be the biggest thrill in racing. That was on a Friday night. Saturday night we came back to Silver Spring and won, and Sunday night we ran Susquehanna Speedway and finished second. It was a really good weekend. That had to be the biggest weekend I ever had.

Kramer was ready to take the next step in his racing career and move on to central Pennsylvania's premier class of race cars, Sprint Cars. Not racing during the last half of the 1970 season allowed Kramer and his father to get prepared for their inaugural Sprint Car season the following year. The family went to Toby Tobias and bought a chassis for the 1971 season. Earl Williamson also approached ace mechanic and Sprint Car guru Davey Brown to help build the car and motors for that year as well. He explained that his son wanted to go Sprint Car racing and asked for his help. Davey Brown recalls: "I remember the first time he started that Sprint Car he must have been no older than 19 or 20 at the time. He was real nervous. He ran Silver Spring Sportsman cars and they had a starter on them. He had never started a Sprint Car before. In those days, by my shop, we would just push them down the highway. Of course, you can't do that anymore; there is way too much traffic."

Kramer was anxious but well prepared for his next great challenge: to beat Pennsylvania's best in a family-owned and -run Sprint Car. Some said it was an almost impossible task to accomplish, but Kramer had other ideas.

2

Early Years

Kramer Williamson would enter his rookie year racing Sprint Cars in his family-owned #73, well prepared to take on the steep learning curve of piloting one of these winged machines. His first race of the 1971 race season would be at the famed ⁴/₁₀ mile Susquehanna Speedway in York Haven, Pennsylvania. In his very first outing in a winged Sprint Car and competing against the best of that era, Kramer would finish a solid eleventh place. Kramer would follow up his solid debut with an eighth-place finish and a fourth-place finish in the next two races, against the top drivers of the period. With the combination of a supportive family and mechanic Davey Brown, it would take Kramer only four races at Susquehanna to find himself in Victory Lane for the first time in his young career behind the wheel of a winged Sprint Car, beating Mitch Smith, one the region's best drivers at that time. In a 1976 interview, Kramer himself described what it was like to compete in his first Sprint Car season.

> Well, in racing Sprint Cars you are in a completely different class of racing—this is the first thing you realize. I also realized really quickly that you must be a lot sharper than when you raced the Sportsman cars. Fuel injection made the Sprint Car much quicker than what I drove at Silver Spring. To go along with that, your reflexes and reaction time must be a lot quicker. You can watch and watch, but to become competitive, you must get on the track and do it. There is a feel to it you must have or acquire. I found myself always getting into trouble when I first began in the sprinters. After some experience, I learned to make snap judgments and stay out of trouble.

In 1971, Kramer's first season racing a Sprint Car, he won three Rookie of the Year titles. Williams Grove Speedway, Port Royal Speedway and Susquehanna Speedway would all bestow Rookie of the Year honors on Kramer Williamson as the best up-and-coming Sprint Car driver for that year. All would not be a success, though, in 1971. During a race mid-year at Susquehanna Speedway, Kramer sailed his Sprint Car out of the track's first turn and subsequently left the race car as a complete loss. Once again, the Williamson family sprang into action to support young Kramer's racing career. Everyone pooled their money and bought a new Floyd Trevis chassis to replace the totaled Tobias chassis car. Of course, when it came time to paint the new machine, there was the obvious choice of color, that familiar pink hue that everyone had come to associate with Kramer.

Around the same time the Williamson family acquired the new Trevis chassis car, someone was joking around in the pits and stuck a Pink Panther sticker on the wing as a joke. The name "Pink Panther" stuck and was a perfect fit for the young Sprint Car star. Kramer would be known as the "Pink Panther" throughout his long career and his race cars would bear the name and even the Pink Panther's image on them. Kramer even tried to capitalize on some sponsorship opportunities with his unique nickname. Looking for an opportunity to get sponsorship dollars for his racing program, Kramer once wrote a proposal

Kramer stands next to his #73 Pink Panther Sprint Car in his first appearance at Reading Fairgrounds Speedway on March 12, 1972.

to Owens Corning, who used the Pink Panther in some of their advertising for their pink insulation. The response was not what the young racer was expecting. Instead of an agreement to capitalize on the opportunity, Kramer received a letter stating that he could be using their logo without their authorization and thus could be sued. His younger brother, George Jr., who was making a name for himself lettering cars and signs at the time, simply added a hat and a cane to the Pink Panther to avoid any logo infringements, and the Pink Panther became a fixture on Kramer's cars for the rest of his life.

In an interview with *Flat Out Illustrated* later in his life, Kramer fondly remembers his Floyd Trevis car:

> In the 10 years we had the car, we put three front clips on it. We cut it up and pieced it back together, just kept patching it. And you know, the car always worked. We would get into a dry-slick situation and we'd be tough. We were always good on dry-slick tracks. The car would hook up so good, but I guess part of it was because our motor program was not the greatest.

Kramer and his father did most of the engine work themselves. The duo would have Bill Gettle of A&G Automotive do most of the machine work involved with the motors, and then the Williamsons would take care of the assembly and final tuning.

Although Kramer would give lots of credit to his Trevis car, it is always the driver and the art of pushing the gas pedal just the right amount that contributes to success on dry-slick tracks. United Racing Club Champion Greg Coverdale, who would race with Kramer much later in his career, remembers Kramer's uncanny ability to run fast on a dry-slick track:

> Kramer had an uncanny ability to run the bottom. When the track was dry and slick and everybody else was up top or spinning loose, he could find the groove. He could find the middle and he was great at coming off right against the tires on a super slick track. When the track lost its heaviness and started to slick up, he was so tough.

The 1971 season was a year in which Kramer would find his way in the tough world of Sprint Cars. Racing several nights every week and learning new skills on an almost nightly basis, the young Williamson would head straight in 1972 with the confidence that he could compete against the best the sport had to offer. Not only were the fans starting to notice his skills, so were some of the top car owners in the business.

Tim Hamilton, son of legendary car owner Al Hamilton, remembers well a particular night at Selinsgrove Speedway:

> Kramer was running his own car and was leading the race, but blew the engine right at the end and Bobby Adamson won that night. Jack Gunn was doing the interview in Victory Lane with Adamson and they invited Kramer to Victory Lane. Bobby was a respectful enough guy to recognize the young talent of Kramer Williamson and I remember that night as being a big deal and a symbolic changing of the guard. Not only did he catch the attention of Bobby Adamson, but it positively caught the attention of my dad. Once that happens to drivers and you get the attention of what I would call pinnacle owners like my dad [Al Hamilton] or Bob Weikert, the drivers reach a

Strapped in and ready to go. Kramer Williamson prepares for battle during the early years of his Sprint Car career.

heightened level of respect from both elite drivers and owners. Then they move into a whole other category. You now know guys are paying attention to you.

While Kramer still ran his own equipment in 1972, it would not be long before some of the best car owners in the Sprint Car world started knocking on his door. Kramer, who had now graduated from Williamsport Area Community College, went to work as a mechanic at Earl B. Lehman, a Ford Lincoln-Mercury dealership. Little did he know he was working for his future father-in-law. While working at the dealership, he met his future wife, Sharon Beahm.

From a young age, Sharon had a love of racing equal to that of her future husband. She was the daughter of former driver and Keystone Auto Racing on Speedways (KARS) pit steward Lyle Beahm. Sharon's sisters, Sandy Beahm and Debbie Beahm, also helped register and score cars at many of the local tracks. Sharon fondly remembers seeing Kramer at the dealership and at the local tracks where she worked the gate and as a scorer during KARS races. Sharon recounts her first inter-action with Kramer in 1972: "My family had a boat and I would go down to the dealership to clean the boat up just because I knew Kramer was there. I would then see him at the races at Selinsgrove and he would always say to me that he was going to take me home some night and one night I let him take me home. It's funny how everything worked out."

Kramer and Sharon instantly hit it off and began to date. Dating the boss's daughter definitely had its moments. Sharon remembers when they started dating that "Kramer sometimes would not show up to work or would be late, which was always almost related to racing. My dad would always get on me and say, 'Where the heck is Kramer today?'" Kramer eventually left after months working at the Ford dealership, when he enlisted in the Air National Guard. Through all the changes, his faithful girlfriend Sharon remained at his side and would often receive letters from Kramer during his basic training.

Kramer would write about his plans for when he got out of basic training. In this one particular letter, he wrote to Sharon, "I tell you this is what I really wish would happen. I wish I could drive for Bud Grimm next year and could get a really good job making a lot of money. I know where I can get some ground and build a garage of my own and of course couldn't you see me and the number 88 in Victory Lane!" As

Kramer's father-in-law, Lyle Beahm, stands next to his immaculately pre-pared race car and matching truck. Racing roots run deep on all sides of the Williamson family.

fate would have it, much of Kramer's wishes came to pass in the following years, showing his clear vision for his future, both as a driver and a businessman. He would go on to open up his own shop, Kramer's Auto Service in Enola, Pennsylvania, the following year and also would find himself by May 5 of 1973 in Victory Lane in the Bud Grimm–owned #88.

Many things lined up just right during this transitional period in Kramer's life. When Kramer left the Earl B. Lehman car dealership, they replaced him with a bright young mechanic named Dale Bear. Bear began his career in Sprint Cars with car owner Harold Hank, who brought a young Jan Opperman to the central Pennsylvania Sprint Car circuit. Kramer would call Bear "a darn sharp mechanic and one of the best I have ever been around." Kramer and Dale would form a magical relationship that would last many years and take them to the top of the Sprint Car ranks.

Also during 1972, after Kramer returned from his basic training and opened Kramer's Auto Service, in Enola, he eventually had his own race car at the shop and started making parts and pieces for his own car. In typical Kramer do-it-yourself fashion, he would paint some of his race cars at the shop with little to no ventilation, making both himself and the crew quite happy at times. Kramer even hired his first employee for the shop. His name was USAC, a white German shepherd, who served as the business's watchdog.

With 1973 approaching, Kramer prepared his own #73 for the race season, which would end up being a breakout year for the young star. Little did Kramer know he would land his first "ride" during the 1973 season, a ride that would propel him to race for some of the best owners in some of the most famous Sprint Cars of all time.

3

Breaking Out

Kramer's 1973 schedule was ambitious: Hagerstown, Susquehanna, Port Royal, Williams Grove Speedway, and Selinsgrove Speedway would all be visited that year. Kramer would also lose the wing and go USAC racing with mechanic Davey Brown during the 1973 season. Fans of the young racer would find the now twenty-two-year-old starting off the year in the #88 Bud Grimm Ford-powered Sprint Car. Grimm, who found success earlier in his career as car owner with driver Ray Tilley, enlisted the young Kramer Williamson to drive his Ford-powered Sprint Cars in a field that was normally dominated by Chevrolet-powered race cars. Grimm, who was from Baltimore, Maryland, was used to success, as he had won five championships at Williams Grove Speedway, four with driver Ray Tilley and one with driver Kenny Weld. Kramer had big shoes to fill as he jumped straight into the long and busy season, often driving the only Ford in the field. The team would concentrate mainly on running Jack Gunn's Sel-Wil series of races, which would later become the KARS circuit. The famed #73 Pink Panther Sprint Car would be used as a backup during the season, and fans would have to get used to the red, white and blue #88 with Kramer behind the wheel.

In the season opener at Hagerstown, Kramer did not disappoint his new car owner. The young driver almost did not make the race due to his continuing commitments to the National Guard. He was able to get his duties changed at the last minute in order to make the race for his new car owner. While Smokey Snellbaker would go on to win the day's feature event, Kramer was able to finish a solid fourth. Kramer had been running in the top three, but his car jumped out of gear during the final laps, causing him fall back one position and finish fourth. Kramer would find himself moving up the ladder quickly as he drove

23

Kramer, fresh out of the National Guard, checks out the progress on the brand-new Bud Grimm #88 Sprint Car he would pilot at the beginning of his Sprint Car career.

to an impressive third-place finish at the Susquehanna opener, right behind Sprint Car veterans Smokey Snellbaker and Kenny Weld. Bobby Allen and Lynn Paxton would round out the top five for the evening's main event.

The whirlwind season kickoff continued at Port Royal, the next on the schedule to have their opening race. Kramer won his heat race, but could not start the feature because he could not get his car in gear due to a mechanical problem. In an odd turn of events, the feature had to be canceled and run the following week due to a six-car wreck that caused a 12,000-volt powerline to short out.

The 1973 season found regular car counts of well over 30 Sprint Cars at almost every track in the area. Many argue that this time period produced more legends and top racing talent than any other time in Sprint Car history. Drivers like Kenny Weld, Lynn Paxton, Bobby Allen, Jan Opperman, Bobbie Adamson, Dub May, Van May, Steve Smith, and Paul Pitzer were just some of the talented drivers Kramer would have to race on a nightly basis. Regularly running up front and almost always

24

finishing in the top five allowed Kramer to sharpen his skills against some of the top Sprint Car pilots in the nation.

While drivers Kenny Weld and Jan Opperman were dominating much of the early season, Kramer was super consistent and improving every race in the Bud Grimm Ford. In the 1973 season opener on Sunday, April 15, at the famed Williams Grove Speedway, 7,700 fans showed up to watch the action after rain canceled the March 25 show. Kramer would win his heat race that afternoon and be part of an epic three-car battle for the win. Jan Opperman and Kenny Weld traded the top two spots early in the race until Kramer battled his way to the second position. Kramer would lose that position back to Weld on a restart on the thirteenth lap of the race. The race would finish with Jan Opperman winning just two car lengths ahead of Kenny Weld in second while Kramer turned in an impressive third-place finish.

Kramer's consistent finishes were earning him many fans and it would only be a matter of time before he would find himself in Victory Lane. In a season filled with constant travel and change, one thing that didn't change was his biggest fan, his girlfriend Sharon. Always there and always supportive, she was willing to help do anything, even if it was writing a poem to inspire her man to go out and win. In 1973, then Sharon Beahm wrote the following poem during Kramer's stint with the #88 team:

> To Kramer:
> There he goes down the straight
> piloting the #88.
>
> In the year of '73,
> he got a ride as you can see.
>
> He drives for Bud and I must say,
> they're doing fine as of this day.
>
> The Bud Grimm Ford runs super great,
> thanks to the crew of the #88.
>
> Every race I sit in the bleachers,
> hoping that he wins the feature.
>
> The track was good and in great shape,
> when suddenly in the #88.
> The first lap he took the lead,
> and drove Bud's car to Victory.
>
> In future days where they come,
> the 88 will continue to run.

Fast and wild the car will go,
and win many, this I know.

Kramer Williamson is his name,
someday I hope mine to be the same.

He loves the races just like I,
you know I think that he's my guy.

Love, Sharon

As the poem suggested, Kramer finally found Victory Lane on May 5, 1973, at the famed Lincoln Speedway. Kramer won his heat race and would start on the outside pole. He would take the lead on the very first lap of the race and was never challenged the whole way, beating second-place Bobby Allen in the forty-lap event by a whole straight-away. After years of fielding his own cars through the help and support of his family, this would be Kramer's first win in a car owned by someone other than himself. Sharon Williamson remembers the win well. "He was so excited he stood on the announcer's foot the whole time he was being interviewed and didn't even know it."

Kramer's first win as a hired gun in the NASCAR-sanctioned Sprint Car event at Lincoln Speedway on May 5, 1973, for car owner Bud Grimm.

In an interesting side note, the Sprint Car race won by Kramer in the Bud Grimm–owned #88 was sanctioned by the National Association of Stock Car Auto Racing, or NASCAR. The stock car sanctioning body was looking to expand and tried sanctioning some Sprint Car events. The concept was short-lived, but represents an interesting part of racing history.

As the season sped along, Kramer continued to rack up top-five finishes in almost every outing. Victory was stolen from Kramer at Lincoln Speedway on June 2 while he was leading a NASCAR-sanctioned Super Sprint forty-lap race. Bobby Allen became the benefactor of Kramer's overheating race car and went on to win the feature. Impressively, Kramer was able to still nurse the car to a second-place finish. Kramer's time in the Bud Grimm #88 would come to an end in late June of 1973. The two would split and Kramer would revert back to

A young Kramer Williamson kneels next to his #73 Pink Panther Sprint Car that he ran during the early years of his long driving career (by Jim Simmons Automotive Photography).

racing his family-owned #73 for the time being, but other owners noticed this young driver's potential and it would not be long before Kramer would find himself in another top ride for the rest of 1973.

In the month of August, Kramer missed a few races due to serving his country and fulfilling his National Guard duties. Kramer was running his own #73 Sprint Car before being picked up by one of the best rides of the era, the Al Hamilton–owned #77. For the remainder of the 1973 season, Kramer would have four cars at his disposal: two Al Hamilton #77 Sprint Cars, his own #73 Sprint Car, and the #72 United States Auto Club (USAC) car owned by Dale Bear. Kramer drove the supercompetitive Al Hamilton Special at Williams Grove Speedway on Friday nights and at Selinsgrove Speedway on Saturday nights. The Al Hamilton team did not race on Sundays, so Kramer would drive his Pink Panther #73 car on Sunday at Penn National Speedway.

Kramer would also have the help of two of the top mechanics in Sprint Car racing. Joe Hamilton was head wrench on the #77 Al Hamilton sprinters, and Dale Bear was head mechanic on his own #72 USAC car as well as Kramer's #73 car. When Kramer was asked during an AARN interview in 1973 if all the car-switching caused any problems, he replied,

> No, not really, the three cars are basically the same. They're all Trevis [Floyd Trevis–built] cars, and I've changed mine around to be more universal this year. It seems to be helping a great deal. The same goes for the USAC car I drive, and it's a Don Edmunds chassis. The main thing is getting comfortable when you drive, making sure the steering wheel and seat are in the right place.

Kramer would be fast right out of the box with Hamilton's top-notch Trevis chassis and equipment.

As Kramer evolved as a driver, the cars were evolving as well. Bigger wings, better engines and better working chassis all added up to faster speeds and more competitive racing. The new design did little to slow the Pink Panther down as Kramer set a fast time at Jennerstown Speedway his first time out in the #77 car, covering the half-mile in a time of 20.36 seconds and breaking the old mark by almost a full second. It would not take long for the team to click, and on September 3, 1973, Kramer would celebrate his first victory in the #77 Al Hamilton–owned car at Selinsgrove Speedway. Al remembers Kramer's driving style as well as how they came together to become owner and driver:

Kramer, behind the wheel of the #77 Al Hamilton Contracting Special in 1973. Note Kramer is still wearing the #88 Bud Grimm helmet from his ride earlier in the year (by GW Photos).

I always had one eye on my car and one on everyone else. Kramer was always super smooth and very methodical. He was not a super aggressive or reckless driver. When Kramer got in an accident, it was not Kramer's fault. There are certain guys over the years that were like that. Ray Tilley and Bobby Adamson were smooth racers who did not crash very often and I would put Kramer into that same category. He was a Lynn Paxton or Lance Deweese–style driver. If you want someone in between, you would have to pick Stevie Smith. He was not as smooth as Kramer, but he was just a little more aggressive than him. I can remember standing on the trailer and watching Kramer and I was like, come on, come on! But all I had to do was wait until the end of the race and Kramer would find his way to the front. He was very methodical. Over the years, I watched them all and have had 50 drivers drive for me. Kramer impressed me. That's why I picked him up. You almost did not need a crew chief. Kramer knew what to do to the car to make it work. Kramer was thinking all the time on how to make the car faster. When Kramer and my brother Joe got together they could sure get a car to work. My older brother Joe always wrenched my cars and Kramer earned his respect with his knowledge of making the car faster. Although things could get contentious at times, you could always see the mutual respect between the two of them. Kramer was an honest, hard-working kid when he drove for me. I trusted him so much I would let him keep the car at his place to work on it and take care of it. He was as honest as one can be. I can still see him in the Trims #25 car. That was during the time he was just unbeatable. How he drove it, I don't know! He would go down the straightaway and his left front wheel would never touch the track until he would get out of the throttle to go into the turn. It was just unbelievable to watch him. Although he did not race for us very long, there was a great respect and love between our families. Kramer was a great guy, everyone liked him! He had a great heart. Had Kramer been willing to leave his family in Pennsylvania, Kramer Williamson should have worked his way to NASCAR and he would have been an exceptional NASCAR driver. I can't remember one time that anyone came up to me about Kramer's driving and [saying he was] doing something wrong on the track. I don't honestly think I can say that about any other driver of the fifty I had. He was well liked and respected by all.

The respect between car owner and driver was mutual. At Al Hamilton's 77th birthday party, when asked to speak about his former owner,

Kramer celebrates his first victory for Al Hamilton on Labor Day in 1973 at Selinsgrove Speedway. Pictured in Victory Lane are, from left to right: Sharon Beahm Williamson, Kramer Williamson, and car owner Al Hamilton.

Kramer said, "Al was the toughest guy in the world to drive for, but he had the biggest heart of anyone I have ever driven for." Those few words from Kramer had much meaning, as Al still remembers them almost ten years later.

As the sun started to set on the 1973 racing season, Kramer would hop into the Dale Bear–owned #72 USAC Sprint Car to try his hand at some wingless racing. The beginning of September would be a rough one for both Bear and Kramer. The two made the long haul out to the legendary Earl Baltes–promoted Eldora Speedway in hopes to qualify for the September 16 USAC event. The trip was frustrating, as they just could not get the car to work and missed qualifying for the main event. On September 21 at the Reading Fairgrounds, things went much better as Kramer qualified and worked his way up to first place in the main event, battling with Dick "Toby" Tobias and eventual winner Kenny Weld. Unfortunately, on the 37th lap, Kramer's engine expired and he was unable to continue.

Kramer (left) celebrating yet another win in the #77 Al Hamilton Contracting Special with ace mechanic Joe Hamilton (right), brother of car owner Al Hamilton.

Kramer and Bear's foray into USAC proved to be frustrating, but that was about to change when USAC visited Williams Grove Speedway on September 22 for the famed Ted Horn–Bill Schindler Memorial Race. Kramer was fast right from the beginning. He set the 10-lap track record in the Dale Bear Special with a time of 4:03:08, winning his qualifying event. The record would not stand for long, as Jan Opperman reset the record at 4:01:77 in the third qualifier. Opperman and Kramer would battle it out in the feature event with Kramer taking the early lead in the forty-lap race. Opperman got by Kramer on the ninth lap and the two remained in those positions until the finish of the race. Many people took notice as the up-and-coming Kramer proved he could pilot a Sprint Car with or without a wing.

The busy month of September ended with tragedy at one of Kramer's home tracks, Williams Grove Speedway. During the night's qualifying heat, two cars got together on the front stretch and started to flip wildly. One of the Sprint Cars hit the elevated starter's platform on which longtime Williams Grove Speedway starter Les Shearer was flagging. Although two other officials on the stand survived with minor injuries, Shearer was rushed to the hospital and was pronounced dead. The event was a sobering reminder of the dangers of racing during this time period and the risk that these brave men took every night at the track.

Kramer would return to pilot his #73 Pink Panther at an Open Competition show at Bridgeport Speedway in October of 1973. The trip to Bridgeport Speedway back in those days was an adventure in itself. Long before a bridge had been built to cross the Delaware River, Kramer and his family would load the truck, trailer and race car on the ferry for a ride across the river. Upon arrival at the Speedway, the officials told Kramer that he would not be allowed to run, since the rules stated that entrants had to have three races in at the track. Kramer pleaded his case to the officials, arguing that the papers said it was "open competition," and how many races he ran should not matter. After much discussion, Kramer was allowed to enter, and would start eighteenth in the qualifying race. He had only eight laps to get into a qualifying spot, so the pressure was on. Not only did Kramer qualify, he went all the way to the front and won his heat race in dramatic fashion. In doing so, he broke the track record with a lap of 21.5 seconds on the ⅝-mile oval. In the feature open competition event, Kramer would come home in third place, an impressive run all the way from the twenty-first starting spot at a track he had never before seen. Kramer continued to impress with his ability to adapt to any track in any car.

The 1973 season would end with Pennsylvania's biggest race: the Eleventh Annual Williams Grove Speedway National Open. To this day, the Open is one of the biggest and most important Sprint Car races in the world. Unlike most Sprint Car races lasting on average forty laps, this race was a grueling one hundred and fifty–lap event. Kenny Weld's record year would continue as he would win the pole for the event. Kramer drove his family-owned #73 car and qualified for the sixth starting position with a lap of 25.306. On Sunday's feature event before a record crowd of twelve thousand people, Kramer would go up against the best in the Sprint Car world. While the day would belong to Kenny Weld, who won the event, Kramer finished solidly in seventh position, well inside the top ten in a car built and maintained by himself and his family. In all, 1973 had been a challenging year to the young Kramer Williamson. It was his first year driving for someone other than himself and his family. He challenged himself and ventured out as far as Ohio to tracks he had never before visited. All the time, he was improving his craft and always thinking of ways to make his car faster as well as becoming a better driver. The final 1973 point standings would show Kramer finishing in twelfth place in the Sprint Car division at the famed Williams Grove Speedway. He would also finish ninth in points at Selinsgrove Speedway, as well as a fifth-place points award at Penn National Speedway. Any other driver might have called the year a success and been happy to rest on his accolades; however, Kramer had a drive to win and win big. Although 1973 was a success, Kramer's biggest days were ahead of him.

In 1974, Kramer would again divide his driving between his own #73 Sprint Car and the Al Hamilton–owned #77 Sprint Car. The duo of Hamilton and Kramer decided to head south in February to escape the frozen landscape of Pennsylvania and head to Florida for the annual State Fair races. Hamilton would take two Sprint Cars south, the #77 with Kramer driving and the #78 driven by teammate Ray Lee Goodwin. While many recognized the veteran racers who were on hand, most in the crowd had never heard of Kramer Williamson. The program even listed him as being from Clearfield, Pennsylvania, when in fact he was living in Mechanicsburg, Pennsylvania, at the time. The lack of notoriety

Kramer (right) and mechanic Dale Bear (left) would have a long and successful career together. Here, the two celebrate in Victory Lane with the Pink Panther behind them.

did not bother the young Sprint Car driver. He prepared to do battle in the five race series at the fairgrounds with over seventy-five Sprint Cars registered for competition.

The first three races were dominated by veteran racer Jan Opperman. Opperman, who was deeply religious and could easily be found in any crowd with his long hair and cowboy hat, put the #4x Sprint Car together in mere days to make the race in Florida. Opperman would go on to say, "Praise the Lord for his help. You have to have someone on your team." The always enlightening Opperman was implying that perhaps he had a little divine help with his Sprint Car. While most knew the name Jan Opperman, the capacity crowd was about to learn the name of a new star, Kramer Williamson.

Kramer would finally win his first heat in the IMCA-sanctioned competition in the fourth race of the series. It was a welcome relief from the first three races of the series. Kramer and mechanic Joe Hamilton

34

could just not get the setup figured out on the wingless Sprint Car for the first few races. Not ones to quit or give up, they kept trying new combinations until they hit the right setup. Kramer led most of the race, fighting off Duane "Pancho" Carter, Jr., and Jan Opperman to win the main event. The headlines in the local paper the next day would read "Unknown Wins Fair Feature." Kramer Williamson was no longer unknown; everyone now knew his name and just how capable of a racer he was.

The Hamilton team also had success with Ray Lee Goodwin driving the #78 as he bested the old one-lap track record of 24.82 seconds set by Bobby Grim and set a new best time of 24.63 seconds. The team would set up shop in the hotel parking lot, often working on the cars in front of their rooms during a break in the racing schedule to get them ready for the next day. Out of fear of the team's spare tires being stolen, Kramer would roll all the spares into the hotel room at night and stack them up to ensure they were safe. All things considered, the trip to Florida was a success and gave the racers a unique opportunity to race, escape the cold winter of the northeast, and relax.

The 1974 race season in Pennsylvania would get started on March 23, 1974, at Port Royal Speedway. Kramer would finish fourth in the Al Hamilton #77. Kramer might have finished higher had he not been hit so hard by a rock thrown from another car that it caused a gash in his arm. With the open exposed cockpits of these early Sprint Cars, getting hit and injured by flying debris was often a hazard of the job, and the tough drivers of the day simply dealt with it and moved on. Just like the previous year, Kramer made his rounds to all the usual winged Sprint Car tracks in Pennsylvania during the early season of racing and placed in the top five for most of the races; he even ran the Reading USAC race, finishing ninth. Picking up mostly top-five finishes in the early season, Kramer would finally get his first win of the 1974 season on April 7 at Williams Grove Speedway driving his own #73 Pink Panther race car.

Two drivers got off to a hot start early in the season. Kenny Weld picked right up where he left off the previous year. He and local Sprint Car veteran from York Springs, Lynn Paxton, were both having great results during the early season. Kramer continued his steady march up the Sprint Car ranks with consistent finishes. His comments during an interview after his victory at Williams Grove Speedway victory sum up his mindset during the early 1974 season: "I don't race for money, but it helps pay the bills.... I haven't made any money to speak of.... I race because I like it." Kramer was, even at a young age, a racer's racer—racing for fun and racing to win every night at every track every time he would strap in and get behind the wheel. He gave one hundred percent. After a string of top-ten finishes at Selinsgrove Speedway and Williams Grove Speedway during late April, and a DNF on May 3 from losing a wheel during a race at Williams Grove Speedway, Kramer would step back into Victory Lane at Selinsgrove Speedway for his third win of the year. During the main event, Kramer took the #77 Al Hamilton Contacting Special to the lead on lap number six until a late race caution was displayed. A hard-charging Mike Lloyd pushed his Lloyd Special Sprint Car in front of Kramer on the restart in a bold move, but Kramer was unfazed and held the high line, retaking the lead and never looking back, winning by a mere one-half second.

On May 17, 1974, Kramer would have an epic battle with Mike Lloyd at Williams Grove Speedway. Over five thousand people watched the two wage war during the last laps of the feature event. Kramer tried both the outside and inside lines and often got beside Lloyd, but in the end would have to settle for a hard-fought second-place finish. Fellow competitor and Sprint Car Hall of Fame member Lynn Paxton remembers what it was like to drive a car to its limits and not necessarily be the winner of the race:

> There were certain guys who had the ability to carry a car. They knew what they had and it might not be always what they wanted so they had to figure out how to make the best of a bad situation. When the car was perfect, I can remember saying anybody could win in this car tonight, but there were nights you would run fourth or fifth and drive your butt off because you really might have had a tenth place car. Sometimes the best races you drove were not the races you won.

Kramer's versatility as a driver would be put to the test at Penn National Speedway on May 19, 1974, as he drove an American Racing Drivers Club (ARDC) Midget race car for the first time ever. Kramer would drive the Ferguson Offey–powered car under leader Lee Earnshaw with just two laps remaining in the event to record his victory. Three thousand five hundred fans witnessed Kramer's exploits that night and were taking notice of his raw talent and drive—drive that he would need to complete the exhausting schedule that would be the rest of the 1974 season.

Kramer standing in Victory Lane in his very first start in a Midget race car on May 19, 1974.

The 1974 season was the first for the new Keystone Auto Racing on Speedways, or KARS for short. The circuit was the brainchild of the extraordinary promoter Jack Gunn. Born John Gunnells, he tried his hand at racing when he was young but found he did not have what it took to be a winning driver. After an eye injury from serving in Korea ended his driving career, he turned to announcing as a way of staying close to the sport he loved. Eventually, announcing led to an opportunity to promote both Williams Grove Speedway and Selinsgrove Speedway in 1968. Prominent track promoter Al Gerber urged Gunn to make a race series utilizing and featuring both Selinsgrove Speedway and Williams Grove Speedway. Gerber told Jack to "call it the Sel-Wil circuit. Then if it doesn't make any money, you can change it around and call it Will Sell." There was no need to sell, as the Sel-Wil series was a huge success and changed the face of Sprint Car racing. The series grew from the original tracks of Williams Grove Speedway and Selinsgrove Speedway to include both Hagerstown Speedway and Penn National Speedway. For thirteen years until his passing in 1980, Jack Gunn elevated the sport of Sprint Car racing in Pennsylvania to a level of excellence that few other areas in the county enjoyed. He will always be remembered for pouring his heart and soul into the sport he loved so much. Sprint Car racing is still reaping the benefits of the professionalism and standards Jack Gunn established with his promoting.

Racing at the Jack Gunn–promoted Williams Grove Speedway, Kramer would finish out May with a trio of second-place finishes as drivers Kenny Weld and Lynn Paxton continued to win in dominating fashion, not only at Williams Grove Speedway, but also Selinsgrove Speedway and Port Royal Speedway. The #77 team headed into June with much optimism after a frustrating string of second-place finishes in May. Unfortunately, luck would not be on their side as Kramer ran into a wrecking Paul Pitzer at Williams Grove Speedway. Pitzer spun right in front of Kramer, leaving him nowhere to go. Kramer continued the race in his damaged car, moving all the way back up to tenth place with a broken "Jacob's Ladder," which left the rear end of the car to move around wildly. The following night at Selinsgrove Speedway his bad luck continued. He was leading the race when a late caution came out, and on the restart, with his car starving for fuel, he sputtered and allowed both Lynn Paxton and Paul Pitzer to pass him. Kramer was able to limp his #77 sprinter home to a third-place finish. The following day he would jump into his own #73 Sprint Car and try to turn around his luck at Penn National. With car difficulties, he was not able to make his heat and he had to run the consolation. While he was leading, Kramer's engine let go in a blaze of glory, ending a frustrating few weeks for the young driver.

With all of the trouble lumped together in a short spell, Kramer continued to be professional and never lost his drive to win and be the best at what he did. Kramer always came to the track and was professional no matter what had happened the night before. He always came to the track clean and presented himself as a professional, remembers Tim Hamilton:

> I remember the night before the 1974 Williams Grove Nationals after racing at Silver Spring Speedway. When we got back to Kramer's mom and dad's house, his grandmother had his racing shoes out on the porch and had pulled the laces out of them and polished them till they were perfect and then put new laces in them. When he came to a Sprint Car track, he looked like a NASCAR driver and that worked because it spoke of professionalism and a different level that frankly a lot of other Sprint Car drivers were not on in that day.

Kramer arrived at Penn National for the June 11 race hoping to break the spell of bad luck that had been following him for the last few events. While walking through the pit area before the race, Kramer found a nickel and put it in his shoe for good luck. As luck would have it, he would finish fifth in the feature event, a turn in the right direction from the last few weeks' results. Kramer's family commented on the lucky nickel and said it was too bad he did not find a penny—maybe he would have finished in the number-one position. Rain would play havoc and cancel the next few events in late June. When Kramer did finally get to race, his results started to improve, and it seemed like the monkey was finally getting off the team's back. A solid third place at Selinsgrove Speedway and fourth place at Penn National proved things were back on track. Almost always at some point in a season, teams find themselves in a slump of some sort. Whether it was engine problems, not being able to hit the setup on the chassis, being involved in accidents, or just bad luck, Kramer weathered the storm and came out on the other side motivated to find his way back to Victory Lane.

Kramer would show up at one of his favorite race tracks, Selinsgrove, to race in the July 6 thirty-five-lap event in the #77 Al Hamilton

Special. Officials shortened the event to twenty-five laps due to a fuel shortage. Kramer started thirteenth and made his charge to the front immediately from the start of the race, eventually taking the lead on lap sixteen. Kramer would lead the rest of the way and win the night's feature event, breaking the four-year-old twenty-five-lap track record in the process. Kramer's time for the twenty-five-lap event was 9:29.1, breaking the old mark of 9:32 set on June 20, 1970, by Sprint Car legend Mitch Smith. The victory was well earned and a testament to the team's tenacity as well as Kramer's attitude.

Kramer would jump from a winged Sprint Car to a non-winged USAC car the very next day as he found himself once again behind the wheel of the Dale Bear–owned #72. The USAC race at Penn National went well for the team as Kramer qualified with a solid sixth-place run. In the feature, Kramer spun the car out, but regained his lost positions to come home in sixth place against many Indy Car and Sprint Car stars. Before heading to Ohio for the Fremont 5-Star event, Kramer raced at Penn National Speedway in the KARS Summer Nationals, winning a heat event before posting a fifth-place finish in the highly contested race won by Mike Lloyd.

Kramer and many of the stars of central Pennsylvania Sprint Car racing would make the haul west to Fremont Speedway, located in Fremont, Ohio. The fifty-lap Five-Star Championship feature was led by Jim Linder, who earned the pole position. On the fourth lap, Lynn Paxton powered to the front, but Kramer was fast approaching. Kramer, driving his own #73 Pink Panther Sprint Car, started in the seventh position and used the top side of the track to take the lead on the fifth lap of the race. Kramer's rim-riding, top-groove style was a huge hit with the fans at Fremont Speedway, many of whom had never seen the young driver race. Paxton regained the lead on a mid-race restart and was able to hold Kramer off until lap thirty-seven, when Kramer used the outside lane and regained the lead for good after an exciting side-by-side duel with Lynn Paxton. Kramer would extend his lead to ten car lengths and go on to win the race, earning $800 for the victory and another $400 in bonus lap money.

Kramer returned home to the central Pennsylvania circuit and posted many top-five finishes in the month of August as Lynn Paxton and Kenny Weld held a tight grip on their dominance of the Sprint Car ranks. Kramer was starting to come into his own and the veterans were

Winning the fifty-lap Fremont Five-Star Championship race at Fremont Speedway in Ohio, Kramer accepts the checkered flag in front of a capacity crowd.

taking notice. Climbing in points every week, Kramer was now a threat in many track points battles, and everyone was having to step up their game to stay on top. Kramer would continue his winning ways and finally break through to get his first Sprint Car win at Penn National on August 18, again driving his own #73 Sprint Car. Winning in convincing fashion, Kramer drove the Pink Panther Special to a 16.3 second lead over Bob Weaver in the thirty-five-lap feature race. Starting in the twelfth position, Kramer quickly worked his way to the front, and while some would say the driver should get all the credit, Williamson gave the credit to crew chief Dale Bear. The two tried a new tire combination for the feature and hit the setup right on the head.

Kramer continued to split his racing duties in the month of August, racing his own #73 Pink Panther Special at Penn National Speedway and racing the #77 Al Hamilton Contracting Special at Williams Grove and Selinsgrove Speedways. Kramer also maintained both the #73 and #77, keeping them both at his garage while the Hamilton crew worked on the #77x. Owner Al Hamilton still remembers those times well, and recalls why he put so much trust in the young racer:

> It's unfortunate, but there are a few racers out there that are not as up front and honest as maybe they should be and for the most part many are, but Kramer certainly was an honest kid. I gave Kramer the whole unit to keep at his house. I did not even keep it at my own garage. He maintained the car himself and I hardly ever saw the car because I was busy with the coal business, but I trusted him and you could trust him. He was as honest as honest could be.

Kramer was earning the respect of not only his competitors, but also fans. Even owners appreciated the clean-cut, honest personality that was Kramer Williamson.

Kramer would make it back-to-back wins at Penn National Speedway the following weekend, setting the track record along the way. Mechanic Dale Bear and Kramer again found the perfect tire combination and setup for Penn National's slightly banked turns. Kramer was simply able to get back on the throttle sooner than his competitors and thus open up a commanding lead. Perhaps the combination of Kramer's running wingless USAC cars with the winged sprinters was starting to pay off as one had to work the throttle much more with the lack of downforce on the USAC cars. Whatever it was, Kramer seemed to have found the right combination to win near the end of the 1974 season.

Looking to improve on his 1973 performance, Kramer headed into the biggest race of the year coming off of an impressive win and was ready to keep the momentum going. The twelfth running of the Williams Grove Speedway National Open once again attracted the top talent from around the country to tackle the tough one hundred and fifty-lap race. Steve Smith would be the hero of the day and win the event for his biggest career victory. Kramer's day would end in frustration: he had the fastest car of the first seventy-five-lap segment, but would be penalized four laps for stopping on the track to replace a spark plug wire that had worked loose on his car. Not agreeing with the official's decision, Kramer simply loaded up his car and did not run the second seventy-five-lap segment. The records would indicate that Kramer started seventh and finished twenty-sixth in the twelfth running of the historic race.

Not one to feel sorry for himself and get down, Kramer finished out the 1974 season on October 12 by jumping back into a Midget race car.

The Super Midget Racing Club (SMRC) thirty-lap Bobby Marshman Memorial Race was the season-ending big event. Kramer hopped into the Meiss Sesco Super Midget and would qualify in the seventeenth position. Kramer only needed thirteen laps to catch and pass the current SMRC champion Ed (Dutch) Schaefer for an upset victory to close out his racing season. With mechanic Dale Bear helping on the car that day, the duo once again proved they could win races in any car anywhere.

For the 1975 racing season, Kramer would set a very ambitious goal of not only racing Friday, Saturday and Sunday nights at Williams Grove Speedway, Selinsgrove Speedway and Penn National Speedway, but also competing in the mid-week All Star Super Sprint Series that would be held at various tracks throughout Ohio. The All Star Super Sprint Series was formed in 1974 by legendary promoters Earl Baltes of Eldora Speedway and Wayne County Speedway president and promoter Wellman Lehman. Baltes and Lehman, along with other interested promoters, agreed upon a five-race Wednesday night series held at five different tracks in 1974. The races were a hit, and the All Star Super Sprints settled on expanding the series for 1975 to attract top racing talent from across America. The fifty-lap races would pay five hundred dollars to win and there was also a six-hundred-dollar payout to the points champion at the end of the seven-race series. The series would become a competition of a virtual who's-who of open competition Sprint Car racing. Over one hundred and forty-two different drivers competed over the course of the 1975 season, including: Lou Blaney, Sammy Swindell, Lynn Paxton, Bobby Allen, Rick Ferkel, Larry Dickson, Kenny Jacobs, Tim Richmond, Ed Haudenschild, Dick Liskai, Doc Dawson, Don Hewitt, Jack Hewitt, Ed Lynch, Sr., Jim Linder, Gig Keegan, Charlie Swartz, Rick Unger, Jim Darley, Gary Albrittain, Dean Alexander, Roger Wiles, Randy Ford, Bill Banick, and many other top drivers.

Kramer made the long eight-plus-hour haul to compete in the Wednesday night series with the ambition and drive that few people have, bringing his total races per week to four, with one of those eight hours away and in the middle of a work week. Kramer's younger brother George remembers the challenges of driving such long distances in the middle of the week to compete:

> We would race Williams Grove Friday, Selinsgrove Saturday and Penn
> National Sunday and then we would leave Wednesday morning for different

places in Ohio. Most of the time, we would hit a Western Pennsylvania track on the way back from Ohio on Thursday nights. I remember seeing a young fourteen-year-old kid racing at Fremont Speedway in the #44 Bruce Karl Ford Sprint Car one night. His name was Sammy Swindell. There was some real history being made at those tracks. This was happening right after Jan Opperman's dominance and Kenny Weld and Bobby Allen went to race Modifieds. Guys like Lynn Paxton, Kramer and Paul Pitzer would all make the haul out to those tracks to race and do well. Rick Ferkel would come in and be super-fast. It was wonderful to see so many great racers from all over competing against the best drivers from all over. Fred Linder was another one who did well at those Ohio tracks. I recall going to a track called Millstream Speedway in Findlay, Ohio, and the kids of the town would be riding down the streets on their bicycles and as the racers started to enter town towing their race cars behind them, the kids would start applauding. I just remember the excitement that these races brought into those areas.

One of the funniest things that happened in Ohio was when I went out for a race with Kramer and mechanic Joe Hamilton. We were towing the #77 Al Hamilton Special back home and Kramer and Joe were just exhausted from a night of hard racing. They pulled over and asked me to take over driving so they both could get some sleep. So, I took over driving and drove for a while until I could hardly keep my eyes open. I figured it was better to go ahead and park somewhere before I wrecked, so I found a rest area and climbed up on top of the tire rack to get some sleep. Sometime later I heard a bunch of screaming coming from the cab of the truck. The guys woke up and all they saw was trees through the window so they thought I wrecked the truck and panicked.

When they finally realized that they were parked at a rest area, they were relieved, but then they panicked again because they could not find me because I was asleep up on top of the tire rack. I got yelled at for pulling over and taking a nap, but I would rather get yelled at for that rather than falling asleep and wrecking. Sometimes I would get home barely in time to go to school the next morning.

While the schedule was exhausting, the trips to Ohio allowed Kramer to race at many new tracks against many drivers he simply did not get a chance to compete against back in central Pennsylvania.

The opening night of the series had a grand total of eighty-one Sprint Cars registered to race. The first race of the series held at Millstream Speedway would be won by Paul Pitzer. The second race of the seven-race series was held at Atomic Speedway in Chillicothe, Ohio. Kramer would rocket to the front of the field and never look back, beating second-place finisher Rick Ferkel by a few car lengths. Kramer found his groove, as he would win the next two All Star Super Sprint events held at Skyline Speedway and Wayne County Speedway. The long, exhausting trips were made easier by the winning performances Kramer was putting in at all the various Ohio tracks.

Kramer's wife Sharon has fond memories of those travels and remembers a time when Kramer would end up on the wrong side of the law during their Ohio travels:

> I remember us driving out to Eldora and taking a nap under the trees, then racing and driving home that same night. We went out to Ohio every Wednesday night for the All Star Series. We would usually take the rig out [open trailer] and Kramer's mom and dad would follow us in their car. We were in a hurry to get home so Kramer's dad and I could go home, get a shower and get into work. That way we would only have to use one day of vacation. Kramer won the race that Wednesday night. His parents took the rig and Kramer and I had to wait for the payoff. Kramer figured we could catch up. He didn't even change into his street clothing. Well, unfortunately we got pulled over by the cops for speeding. Kramer didn't have his wallet or license or anything with him. It was in his pants, and his pants were in the truck and trailer rig. Well, they hauled Kramer off to jail. He explained the situation, and of course there weren't too many *pink* race cars driving down the road. The state police found the race rig and got Kramer's wallet and license so we could get him out of jail and head home. It was a very expensive speeding ticket.

Despite a few run-ins with the Ohio's finest, the Pennsylvania drivers would continue to make the long haul west for mid-week racing in Ohio.

Pennsylvania local Lynn Paxton would win the next-to-last race at Millstream Speedway before the final race at the legendary Eldora Speedway. Kramer went on to win the grand finale at Eldora Speedway on July 6, 1975, and in legendary promoter Earl Baltes fashion, he had his photo taken in Victory Lane with over twenty beauty queens. Ever the showman, Baltes presented them as "Kramer's Court," and there were so many in the Victory Lane photo, you can barely make out Kramer's #73 race car in the photo. Kramer's wife Sharon, who was then his girlfriend, remembers Kramer's Court and the ride home: "Back then, women were not allowed in the pits, so I had to sit in the grandstands and watch Kramer win the race and [have his picture taken] along with Kramer's Court. I think he gave each girl a little kiss on the cheek. Let's just say it was a long trip home from Eldora."

Even though Kramer would dominate the All Star Super Sprint Series, winning four of the seven events, he would not win the championship due to a mechanical failure in one of the earlier race events. The super-consistent Harold McGilton would win the All Star Super

After Kramer won the All-Star Sprint Series race at Eldora Speedway in Ohio, legendary promoter Earl Baltes had Kramer pose with all the beauty queens and named them "Kramer Court."

Sprint Series Championship over second-place Fred Linder. Kramer would finish a very respectable third place in points in the super-successful racing series.

While much of 1975 was spent racing in Ohio, Kramer by no means ignored or forgot his Pennsylvania racing roots. Kramer would pair with car owner Trim Gunnells near the fall of 1975. Trim Gunnells was the owner of Trim's Automotive in Lebanon, Pennsylvania. Gunnells's passion was drag racing until he got bit by the Sprint Car racing bug and started to field the #25 Trim's Automotive Sprint Car. Trim Gunnells was the brother of promoter Jack Gunn, and though it appeared Jack had little to do with his brother's Sprint Car operation, his love of racing could not keep him away, and he did help fund the team behind the scenes. The Gunnells Trevis Craft Sprint Car was first driven by drivers Lee Osborne, Tom Spriggle, Eddie Norman, Jimmy Sills and Jimmy Boyd. They were in the midst of changing drivers when Kramer seized the opportunity to land yet another top-notch ride. Trim's son, Bob Gunnells, remembers how some of the deal was put together:

Some of the best racing I ever did was with Kramer. It was enjoyable. He was fun to be around and a hard worker. I was young and learned a lot. He made the bad times good and the good times even better. We did our own engines so we were looking for someone to supplement the chassis work and help fabricate parts. Kramer liked our car and what we were able to do. We were in the midst of a driver change, Jimmy Boyd, I think. So we hooked up with Kramer.

The newly put together team of Kramer and Gunnells would debut at the biggest race of the year, the 1975 National Open Race at Williams Grove Speedway. The team got off to a good start and led the feature event, despite qualifying far back in the field, before fading at the end of the race. In an interview some twenty-five years later, Kramer still feels the sting of losing that race:

The rear end had come up and smashed the brake line. The pedal was hard, but it would not stop me. I used my tires to slow down and over time they went away. Bobby Allen snuck right around on the bottom and drove away. That was a real heartbreaker because I led that thing for so long. I started way back and came up through the pack and eventually took the lead.

Kenny Weld would go on to win his last National Open at Williams Grove Speedway that day, leaving Kramer only to wonder what could have been as he continued his quest to win one of Sprint Car racing's biggest races.

The #25 Trim's team would finish out the year strong with three late-season victories, a run that would give them confidence going into the 1976 racing season. Despite the strain of a schedule that included almost nightly racing while managing his own car as well as the cars of other teams, Kramer had an impressive showing in the end-of-year points battles. The super-consistent Smokey Snellbaker had a career year and earned the 1975 KARS Championship with Lynn Paxton finishing second; Kramer rounded out the podium, finishing third. Kramer would finish third in points at Hagerstown Speedway as well, with Snellbaker taking the title at the Hagerstown, Maryland, facility. Kramer would also capture third place in points at both Selinsgrove Speedway and Williams Grove Speedway for the 1975 season and finish second in points at Penn National Speedway for the year.

Kramer's 1975 schedule was ambitious and extreme in every way. Three race teams, traveling thousands of miles per week to race, racing four and sometimes five nights a week, all challenged the young racer. Although Kramer won no championships, the year was a success.

Kramer won many races, finished no lower than third in any of his points championship battles, and beat some of the best drivers Sprint Car racing had to offer. Winter would give the racer time to rest, and to help his racing team prepare and focus on the 1976 season. The hard work was laying a foundation of success. Little did Kramer know 1976 would be one of the most successful of his career and one that would change his life forever.

4

The Traveler

The ambitious schedule that Kramer set for his 1975 season would be repeated in 1976. Kramer would start off the season just like he ended his 1975 race season, with the Trim's #25 Sprint Car team. The team and Kramer were happy with the way things went during the latter part of the previous racing season, so they just picked up where they left off. The team would focus on the Keystone Auto Racing on Speedways (KARS) Championship, which would combine the points of running three speedways: Williams Grove Speedway, Selinsgrove Speedway and Hagerstown Speedway. The Jack Gunn–promoted KARS series would stage one hundred and seventy-two racing events during the season at the three tracks including fifty-plus drivers vying for their share of $500,000 that would be divided amongst both drivers and owners. These were amazing numbers, especially when you consider forty-two events were canceled due to Mother Nature. Kramer would also still run the #77 Al Hamilton Special in the All Star Super Sprints Series, which, after much success in 1975, expanded in 1976 to thirteen races in a four-state area (Ohio, Pennsylvania, West Virginia and Indiana). Kramer would share the Hamilton ride with Mitch Smith, who would drive the car at Selinsgrove Speedway on Saturday nights.

It would only take three races in the early season for Kramer to find Victory Lane yet again in the Trim's #25 Sprint Car. Kramer would win the Williams Grove Speedway KARS feature event on March 28, 1976, and soon follow it up with a victory at Selinsgrove Speedway on April 17, 1976. With consistent finishes and victories coming his way, Kramer found himself building a considerable points lead in the KARS Championship standings. Although it was early in the year and much could happen, it was a great start to the 1976 season. By the time the All Star Super Sprint Series was starting on June 4, Kramer had already

Kramer Williamson (left) is joined by fellow Sprint Car driver Jan Opperman (right) in Victory Lane after winning in the #25 Trim's Sprint Car.

After winning the feature event at Atomic Speedway in Ohio, Kramer announced his intentions to marry girlfriend Sharon Beahm in a Victory Lane interview. From left to right are: Miss Atomic Speedway Ronna McCloy, Kramer, Kramer's future wife Sharon Beahm, and announcer Roy Salt.

captured three feature wins and a series of top-five finishes. Kramer was about to go on a winning spree that any seasoned racer would envy.

Some would say Kramer's decision of his life would come on June 9, 1976. After winning the All Star Super Sprint race at Atomic Speedway, Kramer was giving an interview with track announcer Roy Salt. His longtime girlfriend Sharon Beahm had made the long trip out to Ohio to support her man and was in Victory Lane with him when he announced his intention to marry her. Sharon Williamson remembers those days well:

> We dated almost five years and when he was ready to get married, he was ready. We were at Selinsgrove Speedway. Kramer and I walked to turn one and two at intermission so Kramer could check the track conditions. That is where Kramer said to me, "I think we should get married." Of course I said

yes. Had I thought about it more I probably would have made him get down on one knee but he did it Kramer's way, which was at a racetrack. He got a job with Al Hamilton driving a truck up in Clearfield, Pennsylvania, and I told him I'm not moving up there, I have a job at Harrisburg Hospital and I was not going to quit that and just move. So he said well I think we should get married! So that was a reason to quit my job and we moved to Clearfield. Kramer and I both worked for Al Hamilton. He drove a truck and I was Al's secretary. When Kramer was racing Al Hamilton's #77 car in Ohio, Kramer would drive out with the car and I would fly out with Al on his airplane to watch the races and then fly back. It was kind of neat!

Fellow competitor Lynn Paxton remembers a time when those "neat" flights with Al Hamilton were scarier than anything he would see on the track.

> I remember the night in Ohio when Kramer won and I finished second and Pitzer ran third in Weikert's car. Weikert was mad as hell because Pitzer would not move me over in the race—probably because Pitzer and I got along really well. About five minutes after Weikert jumped all over me, I had to ask him to take me to the airport to catch a ride on Al's plane. So, after some joking around, he took us to the airport to catch Al's charter plane. I remember Sharon being on the plane with Al Hamilton, me, and Pitzer, who was sitting in the copilot's seat. We flew into a thunderstorm. Man, I tell you, it was scary. Pitzer and I made eye contact during the flight and I saw the fear of God in his eyes. Every time I see Pitzer we talk about that night. I have never been as afraid as I was that night. We got back on the ground and the pilot said, "Guys, I have never flown through anything like that before in my life." If he had said that in the air, they would have had to clean that plane out.

Sharon remembered knowing how serious it was after seeing the sweat on her boss Al Hamilton's brow; however, "when Lynn Paxton is quiet you know something is terribly wrong because he was always talking," said Sharon, recounting her flight that day.

After the announcement of their engagement in June, Kramer went on a dominating streak for over a month that would leave the competition wondering if they had any chance of wrestling away the KARS championship or even a race win from Kramer. During the entire month of June in 1976, the KARS organization hosted nine races. Kramer would win seven of them, including a streak of four in a row. During this month, Kramer finished no worse than second place. The fans at Williams Grove Speedway, Selinsgrove and Hagerstown Speedways were left in awe of Kramer's dominating performance, and many to this day talk about how they can still see him going around the track in the seemingly unbeatable Trim's #25 Sprint Car full throttle and front tires lifted into the air. Kramer kept the momentum rolling as the dog days of summer approached. He piloted the #77 Al Hamilton Special to two more victories in the All Star Super Sprint Series right in the heart of Midwest Sprint Car country. Kramer won at Wayne County Speedway in Ohio and then again at Lawrenceburg Speedway in Indiana in the months of June and July. Back in Pennsylvania at his home tracks was really no different. Although not as dominant as in his June performances, Kramer would win three more times and have multiple top-five finishes driving the Trim's #25 in the month of July before weather wreaked havoc and rained out most of the races for August.

The team of Kramer as driver and Trim Gunnells as owner was a huge success, but not all things are meant to last, and the owner's family tensions would lead to the team's closing down. Trim Gunnells's son, Bob, remembers how Kramer and his family helped to displace family tensions with their sense of humor by relating a story that took place at Williams Grove Speedway.

> George and I somehow scraped up enough money to buy a pizza. We were sitting on the trailer eating it when Kramer, laying on the tires overhead, hollered for George to give him some. George told Kramer, "Get your own damn pizza." Kramer spit a phlegm ball smack in the middle of it. George stood up and threw what was left of the pizza at Kramer. It landed on his chest. He won the feature that night, and the pictures show pizza sauce all over the front of him.

Although the good-natured fun of the Williamson boys soothed the strains between some of the members of the owner's family, it would not be enough, and the team disbanded in August of 1976. The team would end their relationship with a total of seventeen wins in less than a year, including a win at the Syracuse Mile.

Happier times were had on August 14, 1976. Kramer married Sharon Beahm in typical racer fashion, on race day in the morning, so they could attend the races that night. Sharon recalls their special day:

> Kramer and I were married August 14, 1976. We got married at 11:00 a.m. in the morning so we could go racing that evening. Kramer's mom always did say if you got married before 12:00 noon your marriage would always be going up like the hour hands on a clock. But if you married after 12:00 then your marriage would keep going downward. I know it was an old wives' tale, but hey, Kramer and I lasted a lifetime. We got married, had a reception, and went racing at Selinsgrove all in the same day. We did get rained

out that night and after paying for the pit passes, we went to a little tavern in Beavertown with Ralphie Heinzelman, who was the crew chief of Lynn Paxton's car. We got steak dinners and did a lot of socializing. We then proceeded to Amity Hall down the road to get a room. Well, it seems like after getting our pit passes and our steak dinner, Kramer didn't have enough money for our room. Don't ask me how he did it, but we did end up with a room. Kramer worked his charm.

Sharon Williamson would remain faithfully at her husband's side for the rest of his life and racing career. Always supportive, loving and kind, Sharon defined what it was to be a racer's wife; sometimes a mechanic, sometimes a lap timer, sometimes just sweeping the shop, but always supporting her husband in his racing efforts one hundred percent.

Despite his robust racing schedule and being a newlywed, Kramer also found time to help out Al Hamilton's son, Tim Hamilton, when Tim was just a young high school kid trying to get into racing. Tim remembers his first foray into driving and building a race car:

I was fourteen and hankering to get into a Sprint Car, but dad had different ideas, and Jan Opperman was floating around then and was encouraging my dad to let me drive a Sprint Car. I did hot lap a Sprint Car a time or two at Selinsgrove Speedway and I believe Fremont Speedway in Ohio as well. Anyway, Dad bought a bomber car for me after much encouragement from Kramer and me. The first night I raced it, I believe I hit every car on the track. I was fourteen and could hardly see out of the car because of the seat. It was not even a racing seat. It was a seat out of a truck or something. It had no sides on it. I ran that car a couple of times that year and I won my first race at Selinsgrove that year. A lot of that comes from the help and influence from Kramer.

The next winter, Kramer helped me take the car apart and work on it to make it better. One of the specific things I can remember was that there was a plate behind the seat and the previous owner had a piece of pipe welded straight back off that. Kramer saw that and it was the first thing we cut out of the car. Kramer recognized that it was not safe and made it right. We boxed everything in with aluminum and modified the frame. That car was as close to a Late Model as you could get, yet it conformed to the Bomber Car rules.

I remember the first trip to the track in 1976 and you had to go through inspection and Dory Swisher was driving the truck to haul my race car because I was not even old enough to drive. We got there and were waiting to be inspected and Kramer walks up and says to the inspector, "Trust me, this car has passed." We went right into the track. They did not even look at the car. It was probably the best spec car out there. We would go on to win that night and won quite a number of races that year with Kramer's help and encouragement.

Kramer and Sharon on their wedding day on August 14, 1976. The wedding was held early in the day so the newlyweds could race that night.

Tim's father, Al Hamilton, is quick to add, jokingly, that Kramer and Tim were not even concerned about his bank account when building and working on the car. While most top racers did not have time to help others, Kramer found the time and enjoyed helping the young racer. Perhaps young Tim reminded Kramer of himself when he started at

Waiting to be pushed off for hot laps, Kramer sits focused in the cockpit of his Sprint Car during the 1976 season.

such a young age driving Super Sportsman cars at Silver Spring Speedway. Tim won three races at Selinsgrove Speedway in 1976 and would also capture third in the KARS Bomber Division Championship that year.

With the split of the Trim's racing team, Kramer would finish out 1976 driving for Bob Weikert and the #29 Weikert's Livestock Special Sprint Car. Kramer had such a commanding lead in the Keystone Auto Racing on Speedways (KARS) Championship by the time the Trim's team disbanded, he had the title locked up with two months of racing still left in the season. Not one to rest on his laurels, Kramer hopped into his new ride and had immediate success. After just four races piloting the #29, Kramer scored his first top-five finish at Williams Grove Speedway for owner Weikert on August 27, 1976. The next day at Selinsgrove Speedway, Kramer finished in second position, right on the heels of winner Mitch Smith. The following day at Hagerstown Speedway, Kramer would beat Lynn Paxton and Dub May to the line to capture

56

his first win for new owner Bob Weikert. The team would have multiple top-three finishes before the end of the 1976 racing season.

One could say that 1976 was a breakout season for the twenty-six-year-old Kramer Williamson. Winning the 1976 KARS Championship as well as the Williams Grove Speedway Championship put Kramer on everyone's list of the top Sprint Car drivers in the nation. His stats for the 1976 season were impressive. In the KARS series, he racked up six wins at Williams Grove Speedway, six wins at Selinsgrove Speedway, and three wins at Hagerstown Speedway for a total of fifteen total wins on his way to the KARS Championship. In the All Star Super Sprint Series, he would win three races at Atomic, Wayne County and Law-renceburg Speedways on his way to finishing fifth in the final points standings. Kramer would also win on the super-fast one-mile Syracuse Speedway in New York. In all, Kramer would win twenty-one times before the 1976 racing season was over. In the last race of the season at Lincoln Speedway, Kramer jumped into the #1 Boop's Aluminum Cast-

Kramer piloting the #25 Trim's Sprint Car to a dominating 1976 season, winning the Williams Grove Track Championship and the KARS Championship as well (by GW Photos).

In late 1976, Kramer jumped into the Boop's Aluminum Special owned by Maynard Boop, winning the last race of the year at Lincoln Speedway. Pictured in Victory Lane from left to right are: owner Maynard Boop, Sharon Williamson, Kramer Williamson, and mechanic Ralph Heintzleman.

ing Special owned by Maynard and Mary Boop. The result was a hard-fought victory that would cap off a busy year filled with several new rides, his first Sprint Car Championship, and a new life as a husband. When asked in an interview by *Man and Wheel* magazine about what his fans could expect in 1977, Kramer had this to say:

> Well, during the winter, I am going to sit down, think about it, and talk about it with my wife. I have no special preference of what I race, but I like to race where the money is. You get more recognition, and with that, you get more money. When you put the helmet on, you go out there and you run as hard as you can. There is no use in fooling around. I do want to go racing where I don't miss any shows or have to put up with a lot of hassle. I want to race where there is a nice atmosphere, and be able to relax. I am definitely going to race in the big Knoxville National in 1977, out in Knoxville, Iowa. That race is one of the richest Sprint Car races you can enter. At the present time, I have four different offers for next season. I will keep working full time for Al Hamilton because he understands why I have to take off once in a while for racing. If I worked for a big company that

does not understand my situation, it would not be possible. With Al, I can go racing when I want and it has been working out really good. I can't complain at all. I am very happy and I like what I am doing. I've got myself a van that I am fixing up to be able to travel and go racing in 1977.

As everyone knows, the best-laid plans can often change, and sometimes a path presents itself that leads you to your true calling. The decisions made by Kramer and his new wife, Sharon, in the winter of 1977 would have an impact on the rest of their life together and lead to Kramer's opening his own race shop. Kramer Kraft, as the shop came to be called, would become his main source of income for nearly his whole life. In tough times, he would periodically have other jobs and run Kramer Kraft at the same time. Having a race car can be tough sometimes and racers have to do what it takes to make things happen. Kramer was no different. During his life, he drove a truck for Campbell and worked as a maintenance mechanic at Kraft Foods when needed, but when the Kraft Foods plant closed down, he returned to Kramer Kraft full time and never looked back. Sharon remembers how the whole Kramer Kraft deal came about, why they left their employer, Al Hamilton, and her short stay as an employee of Kramer's new business.

We only lived up there and worked for Al Hamilton about eight months when we realized we did not want to live up in the boonies and wanted to be close to our family. So, shortly after we were married in early 1977, we moved back to central Pennsylvania. We purchased our starter home where I still live to this day. Kramer then opened his business of Kramer Kraft. He concentrated on a lot of Silver Spring Sportsman cars and axles and he did repairs when guys crashed their cars. That is how Kramer Kraft came about and got started.

I must say when we first started out, we were newlyweds and we both had just quit our jobs with Al Hamilton, so I helped out in the Kramer Kraft shop. I would run the lathe. I drilled holes in the radiator louvers that was a popular part of Sprint Cars back then. I can remember one day when I broke a drill bit and Kramer gave me a speech about how that cost us money. I was so mad that I threw the broken drill bit on the floor and said, "I quit." That ended my employment at Kramer Kraft. Well, not really, since I did all the books, ran for the parts and occasionally helped out in the shop, but that is when I went to work outside the home at Hershey Medical Center, where I continue to work today.

Of course, in the new Kramer Kraft shop, another German shepherd was purchased for our watchdog. He was a black shepherd and his name was Champ. He was a dog that would let you in the shop, but when you turned around to go out, he would nip you in the butt.

Kramer would call no other place home for the rest of his life. The humble home in Palmyra, Pennsylvania, would be both a place of work and a refuge from his long travels and adventures in Sprint Car racing. The second floor was no different from any other home on the block, with all the amenities any home would have, but the first floor was pure race shop with anything Kramer needed to build, fix or repair for the many customers who would come through the doors to seek Kramer's skills and knowledge.

With a home to call their own, Kramer and Sharon settled down into their new life together over that winter as Kramer prepared to get the 1977 racing season started off early. Kramer and owner Maynard Boop traveled to Florida in January to compete in promoter Rocky Fisher's prestigious Florida Sprint Car Nationals. Promoter Fisher paid Kramer appearance money to entice him to come run the shows. The series of nine races were held at six Florida tracks, running on both dirt and asphalt. Both Lake City Speedway and Volusia Speedway Park were one-half-mile dirt ovals. East Bay Speedway was a one-third-mile dirt oval and would be visited three times during the series. The other three tacks would test the driver's ability on a surface Kramer was not very familiar with: asphalt. The racers would try their hands at the one-third-mile Golden Gate Speedway twice, including the main event of the series titled the Florida 500 race. The one-quarter-mile bullring known as Sunshine Speedway and the one-third-mile Vero Beach Raceway would be the only other asphalt tracks in the series. With such diverse speedways, the winner of the series would have to prove himself as one of the most versatile racers in the United States. The speedways were not the only thing the drivers had to think about; the series attracted the top Sprint Car drivers and teams from across America with one of the richest purses in Sprint Car racing. Just winning a race would be a very tough task, and winning the championship would be even tougher.

The first race of the series would be held at Lake City Speedway in front of a sellout crowd. While Kramer cruised to an eighth-place finish, Paul Pitzer, driving the #29 Weikert Sprint Car, finished in a dead heat with Joe Saldana in the Bruce Cogle Ford Sprint Car, much to the delight of the fans. The dead heat and close competition on the oil-treated one-third-mile dirt speedway gave fans a taste of the close competition that they would witness over the next few weeks.

For the second race of the series, Kramer would find himself racing on asphalt for the first time in his racing career. With the #1 Boop's Sprint Car set up for asphalt, Kramer would be sixteenth fastest in his first non-dirt race ever. Not too bad at all when you consider that seventy-one cars showed up to qualify for the Florida 500, and thirty-three cars failed to qualify for the prestigious race. After the running of the qualifying races, Kramer would line up fourteenth for the feature. Mother Nature would not cooperate for the rest of the evening and the night's feature event was canceled, leaving drivers to be paid based on their qualifying positions.

Kramer's first feature event on asphalt would have to wait until the next race in the series, held on February 4, 1977. Two thousand seven hundred and sixty-three fans showed up for the third race of the Florida Sprint Nationals. Kramer showed he was a quick learner as he qualified second in time trials with a lap of 14.554 in only his second time on asphalt, just behind fast qualifier, Don Mack. Kramer was a real crowd pleaser in his heat race, coming from last place after an early tangle with another car, and blasting through the middle of the track and past several cars on the last lap to win his qualifying race in dramatic fashion. The feature race, consisting of fifty laps, was won by Greg Leffler, with Kramer finishing a respectable third in his first feature finish on an asphalt track. Making the feat even more impressive was the fact that he did it without power steering. In an interview after the race, a tired Kramer Williamson said, "I'd like to try it with power steering next time." Kramer's performance on asphalt impressed both fans and competitors alike.

For the fourth race of the series, at East Bay, Kramer would find himself on his familiar favorite surface, dirt. Again, a record number of Sprint Cars, sixty-five entrants, would attempt to qualify for the feature event on the smooth one-third-mile speedway. Kramer would win his qualifying race in convincing fashion as the once-smooth speedway became littered with ruts, holes and waves in its clay surface. Paul Pitzer would win the fifty-lap feature event, but Kramer and young upstart racer Doug Wolfgang put on a show battling for second place. With the track being all torn up, Williamson hugged the bottom groove while Wolfgang rode the cushion at the top of the speedway as they raced side-by-side for position. Kramer pulled ahead into second place, only to have Wolfgang reclaim the position late in the race as Kramer's right rear tire gave out. Kramer's consistent finishes helped him take command of the Florida Sprint National points lead as the series headed toward the fifth race at Volusia Speedway Park.

Kramer's epic battle in race four with Doug Wolfgang at East Bay Speedway would be remembered by those in attendance for years. The young Wolfgang would go on to become one of the most successful and recognizable Sprint Car racers of all time. Doug remembers how he heard about Kramer and the respect he had for him from his early years in racing:

> Racing is a small community. Kramer was friends with Bob Trostle and was already winning a lot of races. Of course, Kramer would later go on to run for Bob at various tracks, including the Knoxville Nationals. I was working for Bob at the time in his shop and I remember reading all the racing papers that would come to the shop and Kramer's name was in every single paper every single week. I would read about him winning at such places as Williams Grove and Selinsgrove Speedways and when I finally got to travel out there in 1976, I never will forget seeing him run the #73 car dubbed "The Pink Panther." At that time, I was not running that much in Pennsylvania, but we would meet up at different places like Eldora Speedway or Florida Sprint Car week. At the time, I was running Bob's car as well as working for him, so when we would go to a race, Kramer would come by and talk to Bob and kind of renew their friendship and catch up with things. So, I got to know Kramer through Bob, and at that time, when a guy like Kramer came around, I would hang on every word he would say. Not saying I was like a teenage boy, but it was not hard for me to understand if I could listen to Kenny Weld, Kramer Williamson or Jan Opperman, I was going to learn something, and at that time, I was not a big winner yet. Kramer had my utmost respect even before I knew him personally.

The Boop's Aluminum Special was fast again at race number five in the Florida Sprint Car National Series. Kramer set a new track record by motoring around the one-half-mile Volusia Speedway Park in 18.711 seconds to better the three-year-old track record set by Bill Roynon. Williamson would again win his heat races before taking the green flag for the fifty-lap feature event. In the middle race of the series, Kramer finished a disappointing eleventh place in the feature event of the evening. This would be his worst finish on a dirt track of the series. Kramer did retain his points lead heading to the sixth race, despite not yet winning a race in the series. Newcomer Doug Wolfgang would win his first feature of the series in his Bob Trostle chassis Sprint Car with Kramer finishing in the fifth position.

The richest race of the Florida Sprint Car Nationals was the Florida 500, held at the one-third-mile paved Golden Gate Speedway. The race would be a grueling test of endurance for all the drivers and their equipment. With most Sprint Car races lasting a maximum of fifty to one hundred laps, this race would go an unheard-of five hundred laps around the small speedway. Thirty-three drivers would start the marathon race, and Kramer would find himself starting in the sixteenth position on the inside of the three-wide row six. The race would take two hours and forty-five minutes to complete and have few cautions. The most serious accident involved a young Steve Kinser, whose engine exploded in a ball of flames down the backstretch. This young driver, who would later in his career win twenty World of Outlaw Championships, bailed out of the car and was uninjured in the event. Kramer and his crew called it quits on lap two hundred and thirty-six and finished in fourteenth place. Only one car would complete all five hundred laps of the Florida 500. Don Mack would earn the top purse of the Florida Sprint Car Nationals, amounting to more than five thousand dollars. Although the event was a success, many drivers did not like the long endurance-style format of the race, saying it was simply too long for a Sprint Car race.

Headed into the last two races of the Florida Sprint Car Nationals with the points lead, Kramer was looking to solidify his standing in the series with a victory in his Boop's Aluminum Casting Special #1 Sprinter. In the next-to-last race in the series at East Bay Speedway, Doug Wolfgang and Paul Pitzer were in a heated battle for the lead with Kramer running a close third behind the dueling pair. On lap forty-four of the fifty-lap race, Wolfgang and Pitzer went for the same piece of real estate on the track. Wolfgang ran over Pitzer's left rear tire and barrel rolled violently, landing upside down in the middle of the track. While Wolfgang would be rushed to the hospital and diagnosed with a chipped shoulder blade, Pitzer would hang on to win the fifty-lap event. Kramer was in the hunt the whole race but just could not seal the deal, finishing with another consistent third place.

With a somewhat safe lead in the series points headed into the last race at East Bay Speedway, Kramer could have simply put his car on cruise control and safely driven around to collect the necessary points to win the Florida Sprint Car Nationals points title, but that was not Kramer Williamson. Always wanting to win, Kramer entered the last race with a burning desire to win not only the championship, but the race as well. As the final one-hundred-lap race unfolded, Kramer found himself chasing Roger Rager of Mounds, Minnesota, in the Bob Trostle Sprint Car. Although Kramer tried as hard as he could, he was not able to wrestle away first place from Rager, who was using the top groove to his advantage.

During the post-race activities, Kramer learned that Rager had been penalized and put back to tenth place for working on his car on the track during a caution situation, a move strictly against the rules. The ruling gave Kramer the victory at the final race of the series as well as the points championship in the Florida Sprint Car Nationals. Ironically, Roger Rager left the track before the ruling with the huge trophy, leaving Kramer and the team with no trophy for their victory. The promoter gave Kramer and Sharon some T-shirts from the gift shop instead.

Kramer thereby gave Mary and Maynard Boop a race win and a championship early in the 1977 season. The payout for the Florida Sprint Car Series would net the team $4,430 for their efforts over the two-week series. The top ten finishers in the series, from first to tenth, were Kramer Williamson, Bobby Allen, Don Mack, Roger Rager, Billy Cassella, Rick Ferkel, Lil Joe Saldana, Rich Leavell, David Smith and Bob Kinser—a who's-who of Sprint Car racers in the late seventies.

The Florida National Sprint Car Championship was a huge success for Kramer. The Sprint Car series was run without wings on top of the cars and showcased Kramer's smooth style and expert throttle control. Doug Wolfgang remembers just how good Kramer was at driving both winged and non-winged Sprint Cars:

> His smooth style is what helped him the most, as I remember studying him in the middle seventies when I saw him race. A lot of us guys learned to race without wings because most of the United States was running no-wing events at the time other than right in the heart of central Pennsylvania. I really did not think about it, but when you run at least half your races on a short track without a wing, you learn certain methods to turn a Sprint Car and you turned it with the throttle pedal and you ran it around sideways in a controlled drift, much like today's guys drift their import cars on asphalt for show. That is the way Sprint Car racing was at that time.
>
> When you got into a winged Sprint Car and used that style of driving, as soon as you flipped that car sideways and the big side panels caught that air, it would just dog the motors. In the late seventies, the motors were not nearly as powerful as they are today. The wings in those days were huge, measuring anywhere from five to eight feet long and two to three feet tall since there were no rules on length of the wings. It took a different style to drive that kind of car. The winged Sprint Cars were two, three and sometimes four seconds a lap faster than the non-wing cars around the same

race track. So it was not that they were not fast; the winged cars were blindingly fast compared to non-wing racing, but it took a different style to drive that kind of car.

I would watch several guys like Steve Smith and Bobby Allen to see how they drove that style of car and Kramer Williamson was one I would watch as well. Kramer had that down. He knew how to dive into those corners nice and smooth and use that throttle to pick his speed up just right and run straight as a string out of those corners. It was not hard for me to understand that you can't go down the long stretch at Williams Grove and flip the car at a forty-five-degree angle and keep your speed up because the big wing would just stop you dead in your tracks.

Kramer was as good as anyone I had ever seen. He was genuinely a master at driving those cars, along with maybe two or three others. All those guys that were good were from Pennsylvania. Guys like Lynn Paxton, Steve Smith, Bobby Allen, along with Kramer, all had a completely different way of driving their car, but yet they were four seconds a lap faster than I was when I first raced against them. Not four-tenths of a second faster per lap, but four seconds per lap faster! They knew exactly what they were doing. It only took me running one time with those guys for me to realize that I had to learn I was doing this all wrong and I have got to learn the deal here differently. So, I took what I learned from Kramer and a few of those other guys and I came back to Knoxville, where they did not run wings. I knew right off the bat that if I did not learn their style, I was never going to be competitive. At the same time, I had that in my mind I thought that style would only apply to winged Sprint Car racing, but then I got to thinking that if I can drive my non-wing Sprint Car like that instead of sliding sideways and spinning the rear tires, I'm going to go forward, straighter and faster. Because I watched those guys and was aware of their style, I kind of developed the style of running my car straighter around the corners. I think that probably might have hurt me some on the short tracks, but I think it helped me a lot on those half-mile races, even those without a wing. Even the ones I ran with a wing, I felt like I had a leg up on the competition. Sprint Cars were two totally different machines to drive, depending on if the car had a wing on it or not. One of the main guys I watched who gave me the idea that I better get to learning how to drive a Sprint Car smoother and straighter was Kramer.

After a successful Florida campaign, it was time to bolt the wing back onto the Boop's #1 Sprint Car in March and go racing for the 1977 Pennsylvania race season. After finishing eighth at the season-opening race at Lincoln Speedway, the Boop's team with Kramer, the defending KARS Sprint Car series champion, would head to Selinsgrove Speedway for the March 19, 1977, opening race. Kramer was not happy with the car during warmups for the evening's events, so Ralph Heintzelman, master mechanic for the Boop's team, went to work on the #1 sprinter

Kramer on the gas, yanking the front wheels in the air at East Bay Speedway in Florida, where he not only won the race, but the Florida Sprint Car Series Championship as well.

before the qualifying event. The setup was dead on as Kramer dominated his heat race to secure an outside pole qualifying position for the feature. After fellow racer Tom Spriggle took the lead on lap one, Kramer took command of the race on the fifth lap and never looked back on his way to dominating the twenty-five-lap opening race. Kramer, who replaced Lynn Paxton in the Boop's #1 Sprint Car, joked in Victory Lane about a conversation they had before the race. "He told me I had to win the first one in order to win them all."

Kramer would not win them all in 1977, but it was not for lack of trying, as he would win the second race at Selinsgrove Speedway the very next week. Kramer made it difficult on himself, though, after a first-lap spin put him at the back of the field. It took only eleven laps for Kramer to come from the back of the pack and take the lead. Kramer easily won the feature by a straightaway at Selinsgrove Speedway and set his sights on the season opener at Williams Grove Speedway and continuing his winning ways. The twenty-five-lap opener at

Kramer takes the checkered flag again in 1977 at Selinsgrove Speedway driving the Boop's Aluminum Special, one of three different rides he drove in 1977.

Williams Grove Speedway found Kramer in familiar territory as he battled for the top prize in the day's top event. A late charge was not enough as Kramer fell just shy of winning to Paul Pitzer driving the #29 Weikert Sprint Car wrenched on by Davey Brown.

The 1977 season was an odd one of sorts with many drivers changing rides throughout the season. With few top-quality rides and many drivers jockeying to get in the best ride they possibly could, it seemed 1977 was more like a game of musical chairs than any past season. Kramer was one of the players. Sometimes appearing almost like a Sprint Car gypsy floating from ride to ride, Kramer spent 1977 with three different teams. In July, Kramer and the Boop's Aluminum Sprint Car team went their separate ways. The Boop's team hired Mitch Smith to drive for a short period before Lynn Paxton climbed back into the familiar #1 Sprint Car to finish out the season. Kramer also found himself back in a familiar ride, jumping back into the Trim's Sprint Car for a short period before finishing out the season in his own #73 Pink Panther Sprint Car.

While the early part of the season was a huge success, Kramer struggled from the mid-point of the year on. His last race win of 1977 season would be in April, leaving a long drought for the rest of the year. In a 1978 interview, Kramer commented on the black cloud that seemed to follow him during the 1977 season. "I guess it was just one of those years. It was pretty hectic. Nothing much went right, but you had to keep trying just the same." Although 1977 would not be one of Kramer's best years statistically, along with winning the Florida Sprint Nationals Championship, he also won three times at Selinsgrove Speedway and once at Williams Grove Speedway. A good year by almost any other racer's standards, but not Kramer's. The clouds were about to clear and the sun would shine bright on his 1978 campaign.

5

Pinnacle Years

After a disappointing year in 1977, Kramer set his eyes on 1978 with much optimism. Impressed by Kramer's fabrication and welding skills, fellow driver Dick "Toby" Tobias hired the young driver to work in his speed shop. Tobias was a super-successful racer in his own right and is often credited with offering the first production Modified chassis to the public. Kramer would continue to operate his Kramer Kraft business on the side while he worked at the famed Tobias Speed Shop.

The 1978 season would be a year of many successes for Kramer. He would drive for a number of car owners throughout the year. Many frowned upon Kramer's constantly switching rides throughout the season. His friend and competitor Lynn Paxton remarked on the situation in a June 2000 interview with *Flat Out Illustrated* magazine.

> I always thought Kramer's biggest problem was himself. He had talent to burn, but would get a little lazy sometimes. There were times when the grass is always greener on the other side of the fence and I think Kramer was the type that always jumped across the fence instead of taking care of his situation. That is why he was in a lot of different rides, some of them more than once. I think he moved on a little too quickly. My ride wanted to race more so I got him into the Boop car. They had problems and he left.

Kramer's reflective response shows some insight as to how he saw those he raced with and a clear perspective of his attitude towards them as well.

> Very true. I always think the grass is greener on the other side of the hill. But this racing is one of those deals where the older you get, the smarter you get. Sometimes, there's turmoil that you just can't change. I think when I was younger, I was a whole lot crazier and was looking for something different; that is why I was jumping from ride to ride. I have no vendetta against any of 'em. It's their money and they can put it in anyone they want. Just because we don't see eye to eye, I don't see why we can't be friends. Bob Weikert, Al Hamilton—all of 'em—I go around and talk with everybody.

Whether one agrees with the way Kramer dealt with turmoil or not, much respect has to be given to his attitude that one can remain friends with those he races with week in and week out even if the parties involved often did not see eye to eye. The fact that many owners asked Kramer to drive for them again after they had split up speaks volumes. Most headstrong car owners would never hire a driver back, as most splits were not pretty and often resembled an ugly divorce. That was not the case with Kramer. Often, he would get back in a car and immediately reestablish his winning ways. This attitude simply worked for Kramer. The word was out to all the team owners on the late seventies: If you put Kramer Williamson in your ride, you would win.

Kramer would get a late start on the 1978 racing season, driving the Paveway #5 Sprint Car, owned by Harold Chubb and prepared by Dick Hench, at Williams Grove Speedway on April 28, 1978, after his main ride was sidelined due to engine problems. Kramer would qualify on the pole for the feature event and never look back during the night's race. Kramer never lost the lead despite a mid-race challenge from Allen Klinger. A late race caution would bunch the field back up again, but when the green flag came out, Kramer opened up a 2.46 advantage to win his first Keystone Auto Racing on Speedway (KARS) race of the season. The win would be the first win ever for Chubb's #5 Paveway team.

The very next night on Saturday's race at Selinsgrove Speedway, Kramer would drive yet another car. Kramer hopped into his current boss Dick "Toby" Tobias's #17 Sprint Car to fill in for Toby, who was absent due to running the Hulman Classic in the USAC series at Terre Haute Speedway. Stepping into Tobias's machine would reunite Kramer with former mechanic Davey Brown. The duo would put on a dominating performance. In his first time out in the #17 car, Kramer set a new ten-lap track record in a time of 3:33:56, winning the night's first heat race. The twenty-five-lap feature event would feature more of the same. Kramer dominated the race from the start, never losing the lead in the #17 Tobias Speed Shop Sprint Car on his way to winning back-to-back features in the same weekend in two different cars for two different teams.

After a successful weekend of racing and winning on two hitched rides, Kramer was back in the car he was supposed to drive in the previous weekend's events, the #71 M&K Foreign Car Limited Sprinter

70

Kramer filled in for Toby Tobias while Tobias was at a USAC event. The result was a win at Selinsgrove Speedway on April 29, 1978, in a car he had never before driven. Pictured in Victory Lane from left to right are mechanics Davey Brown, Jr., Davey Brown, Sr., and Kramer.

owned by George Moskat. The team had paired together earlier in the year to win the season opening race at Port Royal Speedway, but had to miss the Williams Grove Speedway opening race because the team did not have a small motor to meet the track's rules. Kramer was again supposed to race the car at Selinsgrove, but as a result of mechanical issues, he drove the #5 and #17 that weekend to victories in both races.

The team was ready to make its KARS debut on May 5, 1978, at Williams Grove Speedway, but the weather had other ideas, and Kramer would have to wait until Saturday night to race at Selinsgrove Speedway to put the new team to the test.

After Kramer's wins in the previous week's two feature wins in two different cars, the pressure was on: people were watching to see if Kramer could make it three in a row driving three different cars. Starting eighth in the feature, Kramer was already running in third position by the third lap. By lap six, Kramer sped past second-place Barry Camp, and two laps later made quick work of passing race leader Paul Ober on his way to winning his third KARS feature event in a row. While it was his third win, it was the first win in a KARS event for the #71 M&K Foreign Car Special team and owner George Moskat.

Despite the lack of a consistent team, Kramer was indeed off to a good start to the racing season. The good results would keep coming as the team finished in the fifth position at their debut at Williams Grove Speedway the following week. Rain would again shorten the race schedule on Saturday, May 13, 1978, as Selinsgrove Speedway was canceled due to the weather. Racing resumed the very next Friday at Williams Grove Speedway with Kramer finishing in the second position to #66 Steve Smith, who gave car owner Harry Fletcher his first win since 1970. Kramer had already won three races in a row a few weeks earlier, winning once at Williams Grove Speedway and twice at Selinsgrove

As he drove for a host of car owners in 1978, the one thing that remained consistent was Kramer's ability to win. Here, Kramer is in Victory Lane yet again on May 6, 1978, at Selinsgrove Speedway, this time driving the George Moskat #71 Sprint Car.

Speedway. He would try to string together his third victory in a row at Selinsgrove Speedway as well, since the track had been rained out the week before. Kramer came from a tenth starting position all the way up to third by lap three of the race when caution came out on the speedway. Upon the restart, Kramer did not waste any time and passed both Allen Klinger and race leader Tom Spriggle to move into the top position. Kramer was turning laps in the low twenty-one-second range and leading when he lost the face shield to his helmet while driving. As if that weren't bad enough, his sway bar broke on the car with a few laps remaining. Persevering, Kramer kept the hammer down and went on to win his third race in a row at Selinsgrove Speedway.

For the Memorial Day thirty-five-lap championship race, Kramer would again have to hitch a ride because of mechanical issues with his team's car. For the May 27, 1978, race, Kramer drove the #42x, the backup car for fellow racer and competitor Tom Spriggle. Kramer had a good run in the unfamiliar car, finishing second while Spriggle went on to the victory, ending Kramer's impressive string of victories at Selinsgrove Speedway. Late June through early July of 1978 was somewhat of a transition period for Kramer. The #71 M&K Foreign Car team that was Kramer's usual ride was now converting their car for a series of wingless USAC shows that would run at various tracks in Pennsylvania, including a fifty-lapper at Lincoln Speedway. While the #71 car was being prepared for USAC racing, Kramer jumped back into a brand-new #5 Paveway Construction car for a few races. Kramer was subbing for Mitch Smith, who had hurt his shoulder and destroyed his race car in a wild series of flips at Selinsgrove Speedway a few weeks before. While helping shake down the new Sprint Car, Kramer posted a third-place finish in the car at the twenty-five-lap Syracuse Qualifying Race at Williams Grove Speedway.

The last half of the 1978 racing season would feature tragedy and triumph in what many consider to be Kramer's most impressive accomplishments of his Sprint Car career. His success would come on the heels of the passing of one of the best and most influential characters that racing would ever know, Dick "Toby" Tobias. Kramer was working for Toby at his speed shop when the forty-six-year-old Tobias passed away at a Sprint Car race at Flemington Speedway in New Jersey. Tobias was a racer's racer and much more. He was a successful driver, promoter, chassis builder, and speed shop owner. Above everything, he was a winner and all-around good guy. Winning over three hundred feature events, including some of the biggest races in the United States, Toby, as many called him, gained everyone's respect.

The passing of Tobias would lead Kramer to reunite with mechanic Davey Brown. Brown was the mechanic on Toby's race cars at the time of his passing, and Kramer was also working in the shop, welding frames and doing various fabrication jobs. At the time, Brown was also building engines for Ed Karwarski, who was the owner of a Late Model team and a successful produce trucking company that was known as Apple House. Conversations between Brown and Karwarski led to the suggestion of forming a Sprint Car team with Kramer Williamson as the driver. Karwarski liked the idea and a deal was made. Brown made a deal with Toby's widow, Mary, to purchase all of Toby's remaining Sprint Car inventory for the team. Davey Brown would take everything to his shop and construct the car in what Kramer would call "the ten-day wonder." The dynamic duo of Brown and Williamson would build the car from scratch in ten days and hit the track with immediate success. Kramer recalls in a 2000 interview the car's being built: "It was a copy of the car Toby had been running, but Davey kind of redesigned it. It ran pretty good." With both Kramer and Davey putting their heads together on this project, the results were much better than just "pretty good."

The crew finished the car just before the coveted KARS Summer National Championship, a four-race series with points given to determine a champion at the end of the four races. The series included four tracks of various lengths and styles that would test driver abilities. Williams Grove Speedway, Hagerstown Speedway, Penn National Speedway and Selinsgrove Speedway were all part of the four-race championship. The team knew the car and driver were fast, as they had been able to shake down the new car and post third- and fourth-place finishes in the previous week's races leading up to the highly anticipated series. In what many were calling the most exciting four days of Sprint Car racing, the first race of the series was held at Williams Grove Speedway. The normal cubic inch restriction at Williams Grove Speedway was removed, making the series a true open competition–style event.

The opening race on July 28, 1978, had forty-one cars registered for action at Williams Grove Speedway, and drivers promptly went to breaking track records. Six drivers broke the one-lap qualifying record

Kramer was an early season winner in 1978 at Williams Grove Speedway, picking up the win in the Harold Chubbs #5 car.

during time trials. The open competition took its toll: the risk of pushing the envelope a little too far became apparent as four of the record-setting cars would lose engines and not make the main event. Kramer started from the third position for the fifty-lap main event and took the lead from Ed Zirkle on his eleventh time around the speedway. Kramer set a blistering pace, forcing many to drop out of the action and lapping all but the second-place car of Jim Nace. As Kramer seemingly had victory in hand, things did get interesting as his motor started to smoke and his fuel supply got dangerously low. In the end, he held on to win by just a nose over the second-place Nace. In Victory Lane, Kramer commented, "You might say we lucked into this one." Luck might have been on their side that night, but the hard work by Kramer, Davey Brown and the rest of the #41 Apple House team was clearly evident in their first big win of the season.

With the #41 Ed Karwarski–owned Apple House Sprint Car team running on all cylinders, Kramer could hardly wait until the next day, when the second race of the series was held at Selinsgrove Speedway.

However, before the much-anticipated second race of the series, rain forced Selinsgrove Speedway to cancel. Determined to race that night, the #41 and Kramer loaded up and headed for Port Royal Speedway, where the weather had not been a factor and the night's races were running as scheduled.

The night did not end well, as Kramer got caught up in a ten-car accident when a car spun in front of the field, collecting Kramer and sending fellow competitor Lynn Paxton upside down in a series of spectacular flips that heavily damaged his Boop's #1 race car. Kramer's #41 suffered as well with a heavily damaged front end.

Word travels fast in a racing community, and many were saying that Kramer was out of the running for the Summer National title because there was no way the team could get the car repaired for the race at Penn National Speedway, just two days away on August 1, 1978. Making the second race seemed like an impossible task to accomplish.

Kramer kneeling in front of the #41 Apple House Sprint Car. The complete car was built in ten days with the help of Davey Brown.

It would take yet another miracle from expert mechanic Davey Brown to have the car ready for the Tuesday night race. Brown worked feverishly on the car when the team got home Saturday night and continued right through Monday, putting an entire new front clip on the car as well as making all the other necessary repairs to the #41 machine. Davey would finish working on the car just in time for Kramer to go out on the track for his heat races on Tuesday. Making the race was a credit to Davey Brown and the entire #41 team.

Kramer earned the second starting position after winning his heat race with the freshly repaired race car. At the drop of the green flag, Kramer sped to the lead and never looked back. Despite a rocker arm's going out on the twentieth lap of the forty-lap race, Kramer easily dominated the race over second-place Smokey Snellbaker and third-place Bobby Allen.

In repairing the #41 Sprinter for the race at Penn National Speedway, Kramer and crew had missed the July 30, 1978, race held at Hagerstown Speedway in Maryland. Even with missing one race in a four-race series, Kramer still had a chance of winning the whole deal because of his two first-place finishes. The rain-canceled race from Selinsgrove Speedway was rescheduled for August 5, 1978, and would be the final race of the four-car series. All eyes were on first-place Kramer Williamson and second-place 1975 Summer National Champion Smokey Snellbaker.

As the green flag fell for the fifty-lap feature, Snellbaker took the lead with Kramer Williamson running second for the first ten laps. On the eleventh lap, Kramer saw his chance and passed Snellbaker, taking the lead and extending it until a caution on the forty-second lap. Kramer did what he had to do and held off all the challengers to take home the feature win and secure the Summer National Championship. The KARS Summer National Championship was the first of Kramer's career and would net him nearly six thousand dollars in prize money, a staggering amount when you consider that Kramer only raced three of the four races, making the feat even more impressive.

For the rest of the summer and heading into fall, Kramer would divide his time between the #41 Sprint Car, racing his regular haunt of tracks located in central Pennsylvania, and running the Mauri Amerling–owned USAC Sprint Car out of New York. Kramer was hoping that racing a USAC car on Midwestern miles such as DuQuin, Spring-

From left to right: Sharon Williamson, Kramer Williamson, and car owner Ed Karwarski take home a whole lot of hardware during their domination of the Summer National Series in 1978. The team won three out of four races and the Championship.

field, and the Indiana State Fairgrounds tracks would help elevate him toward a possible chance at competing at the Indianapolis 500. Along with chasing his Indy dreams in the USAC series, Kramer continued to be successful back in his home state of Pennsylvania. Consistent finishes put him at the top of both Williams Grove Speedway and Selinsgrove Speedway points races. Kramer would win again at Selinsgrove Speedway on a special night for car owner Ed Karwaski: both his Sprint Car, driven by Kramer, and his Late Model, driven by Larry Gorman, won their respective feature events, making it an Apple House clean sweep.

After a good showing in the Amerling #34 USAC car at Springfield, Illinois, finishing sixteenth, Kramer's USAC ambitions ended in frustration at the Hoosier Hundred on September 9, 1978. In a ten-lap semi-feature, Kramer was running well when Joe Saldana crashed into the fence, causing Kramer and Gary Patterson to tangle, ending both of

Pulling double duty in 1978, Kramer not only ran winged Sprint Cars, but also found time to run the #4 Amerling USAC car at select races as well.

their chances to make the field for the Hoosier Hundred. Kramer returned to Pennsylvania just in time to set his sights on the race he wanted to win more than anything, the Williams Grove Speedway National Open.

The 1978 race would be a 100-lapper with cars stopping at the midway point to be refueled, have new tires put on and adjustments made. The race, sanctioned by the World of Outlaws, showcased the best teams and drivers in the United States. On race day, September 24, 1978, seventy-three cars and over seven thousand five hundred fans showed up to see who would be crowned the 1978 Williams Grove Speedway National Champion. With the race being one hundred grueling laps, Kramer settled into a nice pace early on, and by the time the cars reached the halfway point, Kramer was sitting in second, right behind Smokey Snellbaker. Kramer had been in third and racing hard for second with Van May when the two made contact. As a result, Van May spun out and Kramer took the second position. Some cried foul, but in an interview, Van May set the record straight: "The truth of the

79

matter is Kramer spun me out, but he probably did not mean to do it. I know it because I've hit people before and I sure did not mean to do it. The race is over and he got paid for first this time. I'm not mad, that's racing." Kramer's reply to the incident after the race was honest: "I'm not denying I hit him. I didn't know which way he was going, up or down, and I goofed and hit him. It sure wasn't on purpose but sometimes those things happen." The respect between the two was obvious, as no fingers were pointed and both simply agreed it was just a racing deal.

During the fifty-lap break, mechanic Davey Brown worked his magic with some new rear tires and a slight wing and weight adjustment to the #41 Sprint Car. The adjustments worked, and Kramer was superfast for the last fifty laps of the hundred-lap feature. Track conditions started to favor Kramer's signature style as the track slicked off and became hard for the last fifty laps. On lap sixty-one, Kramer went low

In 1978, Kramer won one of Sprint Car racing's biggest prizes, the Williams Grove National Open, putting an exclamation point on a dominating race season in which he won the Williams Grove, Selinsgrove Track Championship and the KARS Championship.

and passed race leader Smokey Snellbaker in the Lloyd Racing Enterprises #56 to take the lead and never relinquish it. After so many years of trying, Kramer Williamson could now call himself Williams Grove Speedway National Open Champion.

In Victory Lane, Kramer was joined by his wife Sharon as well as both his parents to celebrate his victory in what many in the area consider the pinnacle race for Sprint Cars. Kramer would say later in his career, "It has to be my proudest victory. That will be one of those things that no one can ever take away from me. The National Open has gone on for so many years and I foresee it going on for many more." Kramer was also quick to give credit to his ace mechanic Davey Brown on the changes he made during the mid-race stop: "We were expecting the track to get hard, but we didn't know how hard it would get. But they [his pit crew] picked the right tires. Davey Brown works on the car and maintains it, so all I have to do is drive it." Kramer concluded, "I almost won this race in 1975, but Bobby Allen passed me with about six laps to go. I've always thought the KARS champion should win the last big race of the year, and I am very happy to be able to do it."

The 1978 season was a career year for Kramer Williamson. In less than a ten-year span, Kramer had gone from being named Rookie of the Year at Silver Spring Speedway and racing Super Sportsman cars to winning one of the biggest Sprint Car races in the country, the Williams Grove Speedway National Open. Kramer earned $4,180 for his win at the National Open and ended his season in grand fashion, winning his second Keystone Auto Racing on Speedways (KARS) Championship in three years. His statistics for 1978 were indeed impressive. Kramer actually competed in five different cars during the 1978 season. The #5 of Harold Chubb, #17 of Dick "Toby" Tobias, #41 of Ed Karwarski, #42x of Wink Baker, and #71 of George Moskat were all piloted at one point by Kramer during the year. Underscoring his talent and driving ability, Kramer would win in every car with the exception of the #42x, in which he would finish second. Kramer won three features at Williams Grove Speedway, six features at Selinsgrove Speedway, and one feature at Penn National for a total of ten wins in Jack Gunn's KARS series. Kramer would capture over twenty-five total feature wins at various tracks in 1978 and won the Williams Grove Speedway Track Championship, the Selinsgrove Speedway Track Championship, and the KARS Championship as well. Of course, his season was capped off by claiming the KARS Summer National Championship by winning three out of four races, and he ended his record season by finally prevailing in the Williams Grove Speedway National Open on September 24, 1978.

In a season to remember, friend and promoter Al Kreitzer comments on the legacy that Kramer would be remembered for during this successful time in his career:

> I think the measure of excellence he established in his career is one thing that people remember about Kramer. He was always a winner. He covered all aspects of racing. He started off as a kid. He was a driver. He was a champion wherever he went. He won big races. He built cars, which is really unusual. In this day and age, there are pretty much three big manufacturers of Sprint Cars. In that day, it was more creative and racers had more of an input with their own cars. He excelled at that kind of thing. During the Jack Gunn era of racing, he was just plain dominant.

Dominant was a good word to describe Kramer's record 1978 year. No matter whose car he was driving, Kramer established a legacy of excellence and performance that would follow him the rest of his racing career. Many of those watching Kramer's season predicted he would be successful for many years to come. Little did they know that Kramer was just getting started in his career and would continue to race and win for decades.

With the success of the 1978 season behind them, Kramer and the #41 Apple House team set their sights on starting the 1979 race season early in February at East Bay Speedway and the start of the Southern Sprint Car Nationals sanctioned by the World of Outlaws. The first race of the wingless four-race series was won by a young Doug Wolfgang driving for legendary owner Bob Trostle in the #20 Vise-Grip Sprint Car. Kramer finished a solid seventh place in the opening event as a record crowd of four thousand five hundred and sixty-two people packed the stands to watch the night's action. Throughout the four-race Southern Sprint Car National Series of 1979, Kramer would be the top driver from the Pennsylvania and Tri-State area. Although Kramer did not win a feature event in the series, he managed to post super-consistent top-ten finishes. Scoring a second, a seventh, and two ninth-place finishes, Kramer brought home the #41 Ed Karwaski Apple House Sprint Car in the runner-up position in the series behind winner Doug Wolfgang. With a championship season behind the #41 team and a great early season run in Florida, the #41 Apple House team looked to start the central Pennsylvania 1979 season right where they left off in 1978.

However, when the team got back from the early season races in Florida, owner Ed Karwaski suddenly closed down his racing operations. "When we got back, Ed said he was pulling the plug and the team was closed," recalled Kramer. The decision to shut the doors and close the #41 team down left Kramer in quite a jam. Just days before the start of the 1979 season, the defending champion had no ride, and most teams had already had their drivers and team rosters well in place over the winter months. Kramer's fate would receive a helping hand from his old friend and mechanic Dale Bear, who had been hired by car owner Bob Benchoff to tutor driver Van May. Bear extended his relationship with owner Bob Benchoff when the owner hired Bear as an engineer. After much early success between Bear and May, the relationship seemed to sour, and the two would clash after May trashed the #69 Sprint Car. The two often disagreed on car setups, which led car owner Benchoff to release May and still retain Bear to look after his Sprint Cars. With the driver seat vacant, Dale Bear lobbied Benchoff to seek Kramer Williamson to become the new pilot of his Sprint Car. Just days before the season opener at Williams Grove Speedway, Kramer accepted the offer from Bob Benchoff, becoming the driver of the #11 P&W Excavating Special.

Kramer entered the season-opening race at Williams Grove Speedway on March 18, 1979, as defending KARS Champion, driving a brand-new car that had never before hit the track. The Gary Stanton chassis Sprint Car had never been on the track or even shaken down in practice. Bob Benchoff's nephew remembers just how new the car was and Kramer's performance that day:

> Kramer had not even sat in the car. That's how new everything was. My uncle felt a top ten the first time out would be good. Kramer worked his way to fourth and Bob started to get real nervous and chewing on his cigar. He was saying, "Fourth place is good. Take it easy." Then when Kramer moved into third, he got even more nervous and started pointing to the ground to tell Kramer to slow it down. He also gave him the thumbs up to say third is fine. When Kramer went on the outside to take second, Bob couldn't stand it anymore and sat down in the cab of the truck. He wouldn't watch the end of the race because he was so nervous. We had won at other tracks, but that was my uncle's first win at Williams Grove. That made it extra special.

Indeed, Kramer would win the opening race, often called the "Lid-Lifter," in spectacular fashion. Kramer started the feature in the third position and moved into the second position, trailing leader Bobby Weaver. On the ninth lap of competition, Kramer changed his line around the speedway to the high groove and rocketed into the lead. Lynn Paxton, who had started in the tenth position, moved into the runner-up position and made a challenge on the seventeenth lap of the twenty-five-lap feature. Paxton moved his #1 Boop's Special Sprint Car alongside Kramer for the lead, racing into the third turn. Kramer was able to hold off the challenge for the remainder of the race and finish ahead of the hard-charging challenge of Lynn Paxton by a mere second at the checkered flag.

In spite of his being the defending KARS Champion, many considered Kramer's 1979 season-opening win a victory for the underdogs. Many also thought the victory was an upset win since the car had never been raced before and won on its first appearance at the track. Car owner Bob Benchoff was clearly impressed by not only his new driver's talent and ability but also by his mechanic Dale Bear and his mechanical prowess. So impressed was Benchoff that in Victory Lane he said the prize money would be split between driver Kramer Williamson and chief mechanic Dale Bear, a fitting gesture as the team set forth on a busy schedule for the 1979 season.

The #11 team was not the only busy race team in 1979. Kramer, in typical fashion, would set a blistering schedule for the season with the addition of driving the #34 Amerling Racing Team USAC car at several events during the year. Driving was not the only item Kramer had on his plate anymore. His Kramer Kraft business was starting to make strides, and with former Silver Spring and Penn National Super Sportsman Champion Daryl Sheaffer driving a Kramer Kraft car and winning, his business was picking up. Racers like former Silver Spring Speedway Champion Fred Putney also sought out the knowledge and skills of Kramer Williamson to help them go faster and win.

The tumultuous times of the late seventies did little to slow Sprint Car racing down in central Pennsylvania. With the rising cost of equipment and much of the nation dealing with gas shortages, racing went on as normal in the hard-core Sprint Car–rich area of the state. Even a pending nuclear disaster did little to slow racing down in 1979. When the Three Mile Island nuclear plant located on the Susquehanna River three miles south of Harrisburg, Pennsylvania, started to leak radiation in 1979, thousands were evacuated and many left the area until

Shown in Victory Lane from left to right are Kramer Williamson, Sharon Williamson, and car owner Bob Benchoff. The new team surprised everyone by winning the very first race of the 1979 season at Williams Grove.

everything was deemed safe. It was business as usual for promoter Jack Gunn, but the threat definitely had its impact on local racing. Williams Grove Speedway, which was fifteen miles south of Harrisburg, saw races sparsely attended by fans, and some racers would not even come to the area until everything was considered safe. Fortunately, the accident was contained, but the controversial plant remained on everyone's mind for much of 1979 and longer.

Despite the near disaster of Three Mile Island, life and racing went on in central Pennsylvania, and Kramer was no exception. Kramer would double down and win back-to-back features the next week at Williams Grove Speedway on Friday night and Selinsgrove Speedway on Saturday night. At Williams Grove Speedway, Kramer was the benefactor of a collision between Eddie Zirkle and Keith Kauffman while racing for the lead on lap number sixteen of the twenty-five-lap feature. Kramer was cruising in third place when the two got together, resulting in damage to both Zirkle and Kauffman. Kramer inherited the lead and capitalized on the situation, holding off Allen Klinger to win his second race of the year at Williams Grove Speedway. The next night at Selinsgrove Speedway, while driving the #11 Sprint Car, Kramer won in convincing fashion. Although the race had many cautions, Kramer was able to extend his lead on every restart and easily went on to Victory Lane over second-place finisher Randy Wolfe.

With Kramer and Lynn Paxton dominating the early season, many thought the KARS Championship would be a showdown between the two Hall of Fame drivers for top honors. Lynn remembers the battles he had with Kramer in early 1979:

> During the opener in 1979 at Williams Grove, Kramer was leading in Benchoff's car and I was in second and I got a shot at passing Kramer, but I did not take it because I knew there would be more opportunities to pass towards the end of the race. There were lapped cars around and I just thought I would get another shot at passing him later with less traffic. Well, I never got another shot at passing him. I just thought to myself that I was going good enough that I would get the opportunity again and it just did not come.
>
> There were times when he was a little better than I was and there were times when I was a little better than him. We would kid each other about it after a race. We guys who race together a lot would bust each other's chops after the races about who got the best on whoever. One time at an afternoon race I made the car real wide on purpose because I knew Kramer was behind me. I wiggled the car some and afterwards, Kramer came up to me and said, "What the hell was that, were you trying to play Van May?" I asked him did it confuse him and Kramer said, "Well yeah," and I said, well, that's what I was trying to do. It was not my style to move around on the straightaway, but Kramer wanted to let me know he knew exactly what I was doing and he was right.
>
> I remember one time we went to an All-Star show in Ohio and Kramer and I had to come back, so instead of coming back with my car I drove back with Kramer. Of course, he was sleeping the first shift and I was driving fast to get back home. Son of a gun, I got arrested in Ohio for speeding and out there if you had a certain credit card you could pay the fine right then. Well, I did not have that credit card, so Kramer stayed in the car and slept and the cop took me back to town to pay my fine. It took two hours for me to pay that fine and Kramer slept the whole time in the car, that son of a gun. I never forgot those times!
>
> Kramer was such a natural. Everyone wanted Kramer to drive for them because he was just very good at a lot of different things. He was just a good racer. He just loved it; you have to love it to race forty-five years. I had nothing but respect for Kramer the whole way through. I don't think we ever had a cross word, ever.
>
> When I look back on my career, I got to admit there were a lot of people

that I had run-ins with, then there those I did not have a problem with like Kramer, but there were others that you always seemed to have a problem with. I think racers learn really quick if a guy is going to race you clean, then you will race him clean as well. In other words, if you know a guy is going to pinch you, then you don't mind pinching him back. On the other hand, if you know the other guy will never pinch you, then you are never going to pinch him. I will use Paul Pitzer as an example. Pitzer was a tough racer, but like Kramer I never had a problem with him. He never took advantage of me and I never took advantage of him, and that's just the way it was.

While Paxton and Kramer would race each other as gentlemen their entire career, the battle for the 1979 championship ended up not going well, as Kramer was about to go on an epic streak of misfortune and bad luck that would end his hopes for a repeat as KARS Champion. A series of top-three finishes would be marred by several did-not-finishes (DNFs) due to blown motors, gearbox failures and other mechanical issues. Despite the hard luck, Kramer found time to dedicate to Kramer Kraft as dealers such as Budd Olsen's Speed Supplies began to carry Sprint Cars and Sprint Car components by Kramer Kraft in their shops.

Amid the slump came a new ride for Kramer. Earlier in the season, Paul Pitzer surprised everyone by retiring and walking away from racing. Pitzer, who was known as one of Pennsylvania's toughest competitors, called it quits, leaving the seat open in the #29 Weikert's Livestock Special. One of the top Sprint Car rides in the area at the time, the seat was quickly filled by Jim Edwards. Edwards's time in the car would be short-lived as he and Kramer would swap rides mid-year. Edwards would hop into the Benchoff #11 Sprint Car and Kramer would now be the driver for Bob Weikert and his #29 Sprint Car team.

With his new relationship with Bob Weikert, Kramer went straight to updating the impressive seven-car stable that Weikert had assembled. When asked about which car he would drive, Kramer replied, "Bob told me to go ahead and build a new car. His cars are a few years old and a little heavy. It is just as easy to build a new car. I hope it will be ready in about three weeks. It depends on how things go." Kramer was willing to put in the time to update Weikert's aging inventory of cars to ensure he would be competitive against newer, lighter chassis that were now in competition. Although Kramer had not lost his focus on winning races in late 1979, he all but conceded his chances of winning another KARS Championship. When asked about his chances of repeating as champion, Kramer replied, "Paxton has a big jump. I won it two years, so let someone else win it. I am going to race wherever I can."

With the KARS Championship out of reach and USAC and the World of Outlaws making regular stops in Pennsylvania, Kramer looked to diversify his racing. Williamson debuted his newly built Kramer Kraft chassis car for owner Bob Weikert at Williams Grove Speedway, but the bad luck that had followed Kramer and owner Weikert for most of the year continued. The team would not start the main feature due to working out the bugs in the car. The next night, the team headed to Selinsgrove Speedway and won their heat race in a fan-pleasing battle with Lynn Paxton before dropping out of the main event due to a mechanical issue.

As the #29 Weikert team continued to struggle to find the winning combination, Kramer's Kramer Kraft cars were winning races all over the place. Fred Putney had just captured his eighth victory of the year at Silver Spring Speedway in a Kramer Kraft car. When asked about his new chassis, Putney responded, "The car is brand-new this year. It is the best car I have ever driven. If we don't win, we are in the pits."

Kramer was back in the #29 Weikert Sprint Car during the last part of the 1979 season. The team won at Susquehanna Speedway late in the year.

Quite the compliment for Kramer's business and the quality and success of his cars.

With Kramer's desire to run other tracks, the team decided to try to change their luck at Susquehanna Speedway in York Haven, Pennsylvania. After winning his heat, Kramer went on to set a new track record in the twenty-five-lap feature event. Kramer covered the twenty-five lap feature in eight minutes and one second, doing away with the previous record by Lynn Paxton by just one second. The team was all smiles in Victory Lane as the monkey was finally off the team's back.

On the heels of his victory, Kramer headed to Sarver, Pennsylvania, and Lernerville Speedway for the World of Outlaws show. Kramer would start third in the forty-lap feature event that featured drivers like Sammy Swindell, Brad Doty and Steve Kinser. Kinser put on an impressive show in the B-main to make the A-main after he arrived too late to qualify earlier in the evening. Kramer was running a solid third when a spinning Brad Doty caused leaders Lynn Paxton and Keith Kauffman to make contact, sending them both to the pits for repairs. Kramer held the lead until an impressive run from last to first by Steve Kinser dashed his hope for victory. Kinser commented about the dominant handling of his car:

> I knew this car was good enough to get by Kramer. At first, we were lugging a little. Then, finally when we got the ledges kicked off the track and the corners stayed heavy and tacky, I felt I could go. It was quite an experience for me, because I have never missed a qualifying time trial before.

Kramer's impressive run against the Outlaws was one of his few high points in a year that had been less successful than those of his past racing seasons. As the season came to a close, Kramer entered the Williams Grove Speedway National Open as defending champion and one of the favorites in the biggest race of the year. Kramer would come home in a hard-fought third place behind second-place finisher Keith Kauffman and winning driver Smokey Snellbaker. It was a solid finish to a season that had produced its share of ups and downs for Kramer. While his Kramer Kraft business was picking up steam, Kramer managed to finish fourth in the KARS Points Championship, winning three races in the series along the way as well as posting a victory at Susquehanna Speedway. While not quite the success of the previous year, 1979 was in the books and Kramer proved he was still one of the best Sprint Car pilots around.

During the winter, between the 1979 and 1980 race seasons, team owner Bob Weikert made the tough decision to go with Randy Wolfe of Lebanon, Pennsylvania, as his driver, leaving Kramer without a ride before the 1980 season even began. Kramer passed the time in the early part of the season by concentrating on his Kramer Kraft business and racing on a limited basis until landing a ride with Harry Kuhn. Upon the request of Jim Sheaffer, Kramer was asked to help sort out Kuhn's newly purchased Charlie Lloyd–built chassis. The combination would test their mettle against the best Sprint Car drivers in the business at Selinsgrove Speedway on May 22, 1980, as the World of Outlaws came into town.

The World of Outlaws (WOO) was formed in 1978 by former midget racer Ted Johnson, and quickly became the nation's premier Sprint Car series. By establishing a national schedule, consistent rules, and a points system that crowned a champion at the end of the year, Johnson attracted some of the biggest names in Sprint Car racing to run the full World of Outlaws schedule. Steve Kinser, Sammy Swindell, Doug Wolfgang, Jack Hewitt, Rick Ferkel and many more would compete in the newly organized circuit. By the time the Outlaws rolled into Pennsylvania in 1980, Steve Kinser was on a roll to win his third WOO championship in a row and was well on his way to winning a staggering twenty-eight features that year. But even the Outlaws knew to take nothing for granted when visiting Pennsylvania and the "PA Posse," the name given to the local Pennsylvania drivers who compete locally for most of the year. In fact, many fans to this day still break out their "PA Posse" flags when the WOO visits Pennsylvania and fly them proudly in hopes that a local driver will show the Outlaws how it's done and bring home a victory for the local crowd.

In the previous week's racing at Williams Grove Speedway, the Outlaws had dominated the competition and many of the top positions. Sammy Swindell captured the victory at Williams Grove Speedway, while Kramer finished a distant eleventh place. The race at Selinsgrove Speedway would be a different story. After not qualifying for the World of Outlaws main event, Kramer was forced to run the B-Main event, in which the winner would go on to the main event or A-Main. After some changes to the car, Kramer was a rocket and won his B-Main race with ease, allowing him to start the main event of the night on the outside pole position. With the exception of a caution on lap two of the

Kramer delivered back-to-back wins at Selinsgrove Speedway for car owner Harry Kuhn in 1980, beating the World of Outlaws on Saturday and winning again at the speedway on Sunday.

thirty-five-lap feature, the race was run nonstop. Setting a blistering pace, Kramer jumped into the lead and never let it go, finishing a full straightaway ahead of second-place finisher Lynn Paxton and third-place Steve Kinser. It was a popular victory for Kramer, who beat the best in the business in his own backyard.

Kramer's World of Outlaws victory was validated the very next day when he won another thirty-five-lap feature event at Selinsgrove Speedway on Sunday, ending a perfect weekend with back-to-back victories. The joy was short-lived. Although Kramer gave Harry Kuhn his first victory in the #21, he was fired from driving the ride after the team said Kramer's USAC racing negatively impacted the team. Kramer blamed the split on a simpler reason. "They used my running the USAC race as an excuse, but we just weren't getting along," said Kramer.

The 1980 season was a year when it almost seemed like Kramer was trying to figure out where he wanted to go next in his racing career. In an interview at the end of 1980 Kramer explained,

> I got tired of going to the Grove all the time; it was like you had a regular job. You go there on a Friday night; it's the same people. Saturday, you'd get up and go to Selinsgrove. Sundays were either Reading or Hagerstown. That's what I enjoyed about the Ohio deal; we went different places and did different things. Don't get me wrong, I liked the people here. But after a while, it became a regular job.

Indeed, Kramer would spend the rest of the year juggling several different rides in several different sanctioning bodies. First, he would test his skills driving the Amerling #4 USAC car at Williams Grove Speedway. It was the first time in twenty-one years that the wingless big cars had visited the famous speedway. Promoter Jack Gunn made a huge gamble to get the big cars of USAC back at Williams Grove Speedway. Having to put up twenty-two thousand dollars to even get the show, Gunn had no guarantee that the fans or racers would show up for the race. Gunn, who was fighting cancer at the time of the event, would not be disappointed with the results of what would be talked about as one of the most competitive events in both USAC and Williams Grove Speedway history.

The one-hundred-lap event was led early on by Pancho Carter, who thrilled the fans by rim riding the cushion of the speedway until his engine blew, bringing out the caution on the sixty-third lap. By the time the caution came out, Kramer had worked his way up to second place behind leader Sheldon Kinser. For the remainder of the race, Kramer and Kinser put on one of the most competitive battles fans had seen. Kramer was able to pull on the inside of Kinser several times, but was never able to complete the pass before the checkered flag waved on lap one hundred. Kramer commented on his run and the thrash to even get the car ready to race:

> We never got the motor in the car until 5 p.m. this afternoon. I kind of lost count of the laps at the end. I was looking for the flagman to give the five-lap signal and the next thing I knew, the white flag was out. I could get alongside Kinser in the turns, but I couldn't quite pull it off. It [taking the lead] was there, but I couldn't quite get that little extra coming off the turns.

Although a second-place finish would normally not have been a cause for celebration, Kramer was pleased with his run and extremely happy with his performance at one of his home tracks and against the best USAC had to offer.

Kramer would not have to wait long to get back into a winged Sprint Car and win. While looking for a local Sprint Car ride and racing USAC, Kramer was contacted by Pete Sachs and his father, Charley Sachs. Charley was the great-nephew of Eddie Sachs, who lost his life in the 1964 running of the Indianapolis 500. The father-and-son pair owned the #2 car driven by Leroy Felty and were upset because Felty was wrecking the car all the time. Kramer, who was known for taking care of his equipment and wrecking very rarely, was called to see if he would like to drive the #2 Sprint Car in the traveling United Racing Club (URC) series. (The URC was formed in the fall of 1947 and ran their first race in 1948. Still running to this day, the URC is America's oldest Sprint Car organization and was first formed on the premise that drivers would get "tow money" for their travels to various URC events. Today, the traveling URC series covers many tracks in Delaware, New Jersey, Pennsylvania, New York, Maryland and even Canada.) In his first ride in the Pete Sachs #2 at Penn National Speedway, Kramer went straight to Victory Lane. One wonders if it might have been the color that brought Kramer the good luck, as the #2 car was painted a pink hue similar to Kramer's own #73 Sprint Car.

Kramer jumped right out of the #2 Sachs URC Sprint Car and into an unlimited Sprint Car with a team he had had much success with during the beginning of the 1979 season, the #11 Sprint Car of Bob Benchoff. The team had split on amicable terms in 1979 when Kramer wanted to travel more and run other places, but Benchoff wanted to run Williams Grove Speedway and Lincoln Speedway each week. The reunion happened when full-time driver Jim Edwards took a week off to visit family in California and Benchoff asked Kramer to drive in his absence. On August 1, 1980, at Williams Grove Speedway and in his first race back in the #11 J-Bob's "Naggin Wagon" Sprinter, Kramer earned a sixth spot starting position. In only five laps, Kramer surged to the lead and would extend it to 9.27 seconds at the finish to win in dominating fashion. The success prompted Bob Benchoff to fire Jim Edwards and hire Williamson to drive. Part of the deal was that the team would race only when Kramer was available, since he was running USAC, URC and the central Pennsylvania tracks.

Running in so many organizations and on so many different tracks was quite a challenge not only for Kramer, but for his wife Sharon as well. "I had to write a letter asking permission for every race that wasn't a USAC race, even though we weren't USAC regulars," remembers Sharon. Back in 1980, he had to obtain permission from USAC to run events sanctioned by other organizations. Kramer always ran under a "TP," or temporary permit. He explained the process in a 1980 interview:

> If I had a license, they wouldn't allow me to race at other races other than at USAC shows. If you race against the club somewhere else, it was a big political deal. I was trying to make a living. If I ran with a TP, I didn't have to get their permission to race somewhere else. But it meant not getting points for their races.

Going where he wanted and racing where he wanted defined Kramer Williamson's career, and 1980 probably defines that more than any other year in his long career. Juggling multiple rides and racing weekly in different race series with success was a very difficult thing to do. Kramer made it look easy!

Kramer's successful month of August continued with wins in both the United Racing Club (URC) series and Keystone Auto Racing on Speedway (KARS) series. Kramer would give the Sachs #2 URC team two wins in August of 1980. One win was at Grandview Speedway on August 10, and another victory came on August 30 at US 13 Speedway in Delmar, Delaware. Kramer also scored a victory at Williams Grove Speedway for the #11 Benchoff team in the KARS series. As if the winged car schedule were not enough, Kramer headed for DuQuoin, Illinois, to compete in the Tony Bettenhausen 100. In only his second time driving a USAC car that year, Kramer finished the USAC 100-lap event piloting the #4 Amerling USAC car to a seventh-place finishing position.

When driving a winged Sprint Car, Kramer was dead set on competing for the win; however, when it came to USAC racing in the Midwest, Kramer had a slightly different perspective towards his finishing position:

> I'm just going to concentrate on finishing the race. In these kinds of races, if you can make the main show and finish, you've done a heck of a job. I learned a long time ago that you're never going to win if you don't finish, so you have to concentrate on that. The last 15 to 20 laps are where you try to keep it together and finish in a good position. We have the car ready to go. We went to a wider front end because those tracks are slicker out there. I

found that out when I was out there before. It's still a strange car on a strange track and you just have to get lucky. I'm just hoping to get lucky.

Kramer and the Amerling team made the tow out to Indiana for one of the biggest races of the year on September 6, 1980. The Hoosier 100 at the Indiana State Fair attracts the top drivers from across the country. Just making the field is a very big deal. The entry list is a virtual list of legends with names like A.J. Foyt, Doug Wolfgang, Frankie Schneider, Joe Saldana, Rich Vogler, Jan Opperman, Sheldon Kinser and many, many others entered in the 1980 race. Kramer would not only qualify and make the race, but he would also score a very impressive eighth-place finish in the one-hundred-lap race. Sharon Williamson remembers his finish that day and his excitement of finishing in front of some of the best racers in the business:

> He was so excited that he finished and finished so high up in the standings. He was especially proud of finishing in front of A.J. Foyt. Even though A.J. had problems during the race with his engine, Kramer said, "At least I can say I beat A.J. Foyt one time." He enjoyed competing against those guys.

Continuing to race anywhere at any time, Kramer would finally get a chance to drive a Sprint Car for his friend and legendary car builder and owner, Bob Trostle, on October 5, 1980, at Mason City, Iowa. Kramer drove the #20 Vise-Grip–sponsored car straight to Victory Lane in his first try. Kramer's friendship with Trostle, along with his driving and mechanical abilities, would lead to Kramer's racing more for Trostle later in his career, including several trips to race in Australia. The combo also would compete towards the end of the race season at the famed Syracuse Mile on October 11, 1980, in the Syracuse Super Nationals Sprint Car race. Again driving the famed #20 Trostle car, Kramer would give car owner Trostle a solid sixth-place finish on the super-fast one-mile oval. Fellow competitor Dave Kelly finished in twentieth place the same day driving a Kramer Kraft chassis Sprint Car, putting Kramer in the unique spot of not only being a top driver but also a top chassis builder during the week's competition.

Many people know Kramer for being a versatile racer, jumping from a winged Sprint Car to a non-winged Sprint Car, but few know he also piloted Modified race cars as well. Just a day after competing in the Sprint Car race, Kramer ended his 1980 season on October 12 by racing the #10K Modified owned by Tim Hatt at the famed one-mile

New York State Fairgrounds in Syracuse, New York. The Schaefer 200 was the premier Modified event of the year and attracted drivers from all over to tackle the super-fast one-mile dirt track. Well over one hundred cars tried to qualify for the fifty-five-car starting grid. Kramer, driving an unfamiliar machine, qualified for the race in the forty-fourth position, an impressive feat as many of the top Modified drivers failed to make the big race in what many considered to be a turning point year for Modified racing.

Gary Balough would dominate the Schaefer 200 in the #112 Kenny Weld–built Modified. Kenny Weld, the same Weld whom Kramer battled early in his Sprint Car career, built a radically designed Modified dubbed "The Orgasmatron." The controversial car would become known by fans as "The Batmobile" because of its stunning, wide, ground effects–style body. Kenny Weld, the driver, had become Kenny Weld, the builder, and with his outside-the-box thinking and creativity Weld built some of the most radically designed Modified and Sprint Cars of the time. While the day belonged to driver Balough and car builder

Sitting on the #10 Modified, Kramer awaits the start of the 1980 Schaefer 200 held at Syracuse, New York.

Weld, Kramer in a more conventional style Modified for that time finished a respectable twenty-ninth position. Once again, Kramer proved he could drive any type of car on any type of track. Although not winning the race, Kramer had a front-row seat during what some would argue was the most pivotal year in Modified racing history.

Kramer ended 1980 with eight wins in four different Sprint Car series: one win in the World of Outlaws series; one win for Bob Trostle in the Midwest; three wins in Pennsylvania's KARS series; and three wins in the United Racing Club (URC) series. Along with the wins, Kramer had a successful year in USAC competition with three top-ten finishes including a runner-up finish at Williams Grove Speedway. While 1980 had been a successful year for Kramer, both on the track with wins in several different series and off the track with the success of Kramer Kraft, the next few years would be very lean times.

Indeed, 1980 was a time of great change. A big change in central Pennsylvania was the passing of promoter Jack Gunn in 1980. Gunn was one of the premier promoters in the nation in the 1970s, and Kramer was one of his most dominant drivers and stars during that time. In 1968, Gunn was named Promoter of the Year by RPM, and without his leadership, Sprint Car racing in Pennsylvania would certainly look very different than it does today. To this day, Gunn is remembered as a giant among the Sprint Car racing community and his contributions are not forgotten.

6

Lean Years

Kramer started the 1981 season in the familiar #11 Bob Benchoff Sprint Car with old friend Dale Bear turning the wrenches. With a host of mechanical problems to start the year, the team finally hit their stride on May 16, 1981, at Lincoln Speedway. With a large field of thirty-plus Sprint Cars, Kramer qualified in eleventh position. At the start of the twenty-five-lap Super-Sprint feature it took only three laps for Kramer to rocket into the second position. The very next lap, Kramer passed leader Larry Krimes and extended his lead to 3.5 seconds by the fall of the checkered flag, ending a winless streak at Lincoln Speedway that dated back to October 10, 1976.

Controversy would blanket Kramer's next win just a few days later on May 22, 1981, at Williams Grove Speedway. Kramer would win a real nail-biter with Smokey Snellbaker in the thirty-five-lap event. In a side-by-side battle, Kramer edged out Snellbaker by just a car length. The controversy came after the race when Kramer refused to pull his Sprint Car into Victory Lane and went straight to the trailer. Kramer's wife Sharon, who had been a faithful employee for thirteen seasons at Williams Grove Speedway when it was promoted by Jack Gunn, was let go with no reason by new promoters Nick Turro and Robert Jones. Standing by his wife, Kramer refused to show up in Victory Lane as a sign of silent protest. When Kramer went to the payoff window to retrieve his night's winnings of $1200 from the track, he was in for a surprise. Sharon recalls the situation and tells the tale in her own words:

> After Jack Gunn died, I got fired because the new management didn't want me working there since I was married to Kramer and he was a driver. Kramer won the race at Williams Grove the Friday night after I got fired. To show his anger against firing me, he didn't go to Victory Lane. He realized afterwards that he shouldn't have taken it out on the fans but just wanted to

show the management. When he went to get his payoff, it was all in one-dollar bills in a shoebox.

Many in the crowd misinterpreted the protest as bad sportsmanship, so Kramer took out a newspaper ad explaining his actions. The ad read, "My deepest apologies to the FANS who attended Williams Grove on Friday, May 22nd. I, in no way, meant to be discourteous to the fans but because of an irreconcilable difference with the promoters, I chose not to appear in Victory Lane. Sincerely, Kramer Williamson." In his own way, Kramer made it clear that he would not stand for his wife to be wronged, and he gained much respect for taking a stand with his silent protest.

Always on the cutting edge of what was new in racing, Kramer bought a new Bell XFM-1 helmet to wear while on a trip to Indianapolis. The new helmet was mostly worn by Formula One racers at the time and was not only very rare to find but also a very expensive purchase. Never one to put a price on safety, Kramer put his new helmet to the

Kramer giving the L.P.S. team their first win of the 1981 season at Selinsgrove Speedway on August 8, 1981.

test when his recent good luck and win streak turned into a month of hard luck and many accidents.

Kramer's bad luck would start at Williams Grove Speedway, where he ended up upside down, and continue at Penn National Speedway, where Kramer rolled several times in spectacular fashion and ended up on the back straightaway wall. Kramer escaped injury in both accidents, but the Bob Benchoff #11 was not so lucky, and was almost a complete loss. The old wives' tale of things happening in threes proved to be true when Kramer hopped into the #18 Globe URC Sprint Car for a URC event at Grandview. Going into the corner at speed, Kramer's car caught a rut on the track, sending his car into yet another series of wild flips. It was an uncharacteristically long few weeks for Kramer, who was well known for staying out of trouble on the track.

While rebuilding the Benchoff #11 Sprinter, Kramer found time to jump back into the #4 Amerling USAC car for the USAC race at Williams Grove Speedway honoring the late promoter Jack Gunn. Kramer started in a solid seventh position, but succumbed to early engine problems that relegated him to a nineteenth-place finishing position, still in the money, but obviously not the result Kramer wanted.

A mid-season bright spot happened on August 8, 1981, when Kramer was asked to drive the #5 L.P.S. Racers Sprint Car at Selinsgrove Speedway. Qualifying twelfth in a car that he had never driven before, Kramer set his sights on charging to the front of the pack on a track that was one of his favorites. A late race caution on lap eighteen gave Kramer the break he needed, bunching the field up tight as he moved into the third position. Kramer moved into second place, setting his sights on the leader of the race, Maynard Yingst. On the last turn of the last lap in the twenty-five-lap race, Kramer made his move, pulling alongside Yingst and finishing just a few inches ahead of him at the waving of the checkered flag. The victory was the first for the L.P.S. Sprint Car team that year and the first for Kramer at Selinsgrove Speedway that season as well. The impressive performance would lead to Kramer's driving the #5 L.P.S. Sprint Car during the remainder of the season.

Kramer ended his 1981 season driving for Maynard Boop at the Syracuse Mile, again making the show and finishing in the thirty-ninth position. When the whirlwind year of 1981 came to a close, Kramer only had three wins to show, but nothing could prepare him for what would be his leanest year in racing yet in 1982.

While 1982 would be one of Kramer's least successful years in his racing life, it would be one of the happiest in his personal life. Kramer and Sharon Williamson welcomed a baby boy, Kurtis Kramer Williamson, into the world on May 11, 1982. With the welcome addition to their family, Kramer continued to focus on his Kramer Kraft business to make ends meet while he struggled to find his place in racing. Sharon remembers the frustrating year:

> This was one of those years when nothing went right. It was the first year in Kramer's racing career that he did not win a feature race. He was leading many races, but with a lap or two to go, some misfortunate thing would happen. In the early 1980s, we just were not doing that well. The rides just were not available here.

Fellow competitor Lynn Paxton knows the ups and downs of racing well and compares racing to a big ball.

> There are times you are on the bottom and there are times you are on the rise. There is a little while you are on the top and there is a time when you are going down. The hardest thing to do is stay on top. Everyone always asks me, "What's your best win?" I always say your best win has to be your first. I speak to a lot of people that raced for thirteen or fifteen years but never won and I tell them that they are lucky. They always say, "What do you mean?" I said the problem is once you win no one is satisfied with second place. You can't be. Your fans are your worst enemies. There are nights where the car is really good and you win and then the next week or the next night you run fourth but you ran harder to run fourth than you did to win because the car was off a little or something. The fans come up and say what is wrong because they expect you to win every race. I had a guy come up to me one time and say that I had won a lot of races and I reminded him I lost a hell of a lot more than I ever won and that's just the way it is.

The likeable Kramer Williamson had driven for every top ride in central Pennsylvania, and while most owners would have him back in a second, they either had a current driver or their plans just did not mesh with Kramer's. The lack of a ride coupled with the monotony of racing the same tracks in central Pennsylvania week in and week out led Kramer to the western part of the state for the 1982 season. Kramer drove the Frank Crash #46 Sharon Speedway–sponsored ride in the western Pennsylvania and eastern Ohio circuit. Kramer, Sharon and newborn Kurtis would make a weekend out of their four-hour trips west, staying in their motorhome and enjoying the races.

Although Kramer dominated many of the races, mechanical failure, crashes, and all-around bad luck kept him out of Victory Lane for his first winless season ever. While to some fans it seemed like Kramer had been racing forever and it may be time for him to hang up the helmet, the thought never crossed Kramer's mind. In reality, Kramer was just thirty-two years old. It just seemed like he had been racing forever because he got his start racing full-size race cars in 1969 at the age of eighteen. Now a seasoned, successful veteran, Kramer headed into 1983 with renewed optimism to reignite his career and reestablish his winning ways.

On June 11, 1983, for the first time in nearly two years, Kramer Williamson would win a feature Sprint Car event. Kramer drove the unique Bob Trostle creation owned by the Fiore family to victory in the URC series at what would become one of his favorite race tracks later in his career, US 13 Speedway in Delmar, Delaware. So unusual was his Trostle–built Sprint Car that only one other existed, and that one was owned by Bob Trostle himself for use at his home track in Knoxville, Iowa. While most Sprint Cars ran torsion bars on all four corners of the car, the Trostle car ran a four coilover shock and spring package on each corner of the car, making it an innovative experiment in the Sprint Car world. The car was nicknamed the "pogo-stick" by Kramer because of the way it leaped past the competition and dominated the race, winning by a full straightaway.

Before the night's events, Kramer won the URC club's weekly raffle for a cooler that was fully stocked with ice-cold beer. That, coupled with the end of the long drought since last winning a race, provided quite the celebration in the pits that night. With the immaculate #8 Fiore car in Victory Lane, the car owner made sure everyone knew the team was running to win races and not a championship by saying, "Keeping the car takes only labor, and that's cheap. Going fast is what costs." The team would only run Saturday races and skip all the Sunday shows, finding that it was too hard for Monday's work, since the team had to make the tow all the way from Connecticut. It was a welcome win for the former KARS champion.

While moonlighting in the URC driving the Fiore #8 from time to time, back in central Pennsylvania, Kramer was finding it hard to nail down a consistent ride for the season. In the early season, Kramer drove the #11 of Bob Benchoff, the #46 owned by the Crash brothers, the #97 owned by Ed Kehan and the #92 owned by Sam Armstrong. Kramer also had plans to continue to drive the #46 for Frank Crash in the Ohio

Kramer (holding the checkered flag) shakes the hand of US 13 Speedway owner Bill Cathell as members of the #8 Fiore team look on after their win in the URC feature on June 11, 1983.

and western Pennsylvania race circuit. Back in his own garage, Kramer was also constructing his own Sprint Car for backup and future races.

Of course, by his side during this busy time was his faithful wife Sharon and his now thirteen-month-old son Kurtis, whom Kramer had now named "the Hurricane." "Turn him loose in the living room for five minutes and it looks like a hurricane went through the place," said Kramer.

On July 3, 1983, his competitors would think they had been hit by a hurricane when Kramer entered the special holiday race at Williams Grove Speedway in the #92 Sam Armstrong–owned Sprint Car, wrenched on by Mike and Charlie Lloyd. Kramer would start in the eleventh position and took the lead on lap fourteen on his way to an impressive victory and a new track record. The twenty-five lap race was run nonstop in nine minutes and fifty-eight seconds, breaking the previous record set by Jan Opperman. In Victory Lane, both Kramer and owner Sam Armstrong were ecstatic. The win was the first ever for the owner Armstrong, who said, "I couldn't do it when I was driving, so I went this route, and it feels good. If you're gonna win a race, right here is the place to do it."

If the owner was feeling good, the driver was feeling even better. A smiling Kramer said in the Victory Lane interview,

> Man, does this win feel good all over. I needed this one, as it's been a long dry spell for me. I would like to thank Charlie and Mike Lloyd as they really work on this car and to Sam and Cathy Armstrong, the owners. Things just went our way tonight as it was that kind of race with the track dry and everything, but I'll take it. By the way, I had my son Kurtis, who is thirteen months old, in Victory Lane with me tonight, which was the first time for that, and it will be a very memorable moment for us all.

The win brought an end to the dominance of Bobby Davis, who was on an eight race win streak in the #29 Weikert Sprint Car. Kramer was enjoying another busy year running both in the unlimited and the

On July 3, 1983, Kramer set a new track record at Williams Grove on his way to winning the feature event in the #92 owned by Sam Armstrong. The win was the first ever for owner Armstrong. Kramer is joined in Victory Lane by wife Sharon and son Kurtis.

limited Sprint Cars of the United Racing Club (URC). The big differences in the cars made it difficult for most drivers to make the switch from one car to the other, but as Kramer explained, he had little problem driving both.

> If they're hooked up right, it's easy to adjust. URC cars are the same type of car, just a little different. URC cars are generally a little looser, a little more touchy. I've driven for a lot of different people so switching cars is something I have gotten used to. My philosophy is just kinda simple, really. I just get in and keep plugging away at it. I'm not a very exciting driver. I don't make a lot of hairy moves. I mean, if the car's right and everything, I might, but mostly I don't. The thing is, before you can win, you gotta finish, so you just don't give up. You might have a guy running faster than you, but you can't worry about it. You just keep plugging away. I just go out there and run as hard as I can for as long as I can and just hope everything works out.

Besides jumping from car to car, Kramer was enjoying the freshness of jumping around different tracks he had never been to with his new URC ride. The gypsy lifestyle of traveling all the time and seeing new things intrigued Kramer and he began to find the time on the road very enjoyable. "I like jumping around to a lot of different tracks," said Kramer. "I've been doing a lot more running, but I enjoy it."

Kramer was indeed enjoying life in 1983 both on and off the track. Finding success again on the speedways, coupled with the joy of his now one-year-old son Kurtis, certainly kept Kramer on the go. The multifaceted Kramer was also enjoying a huge success building winning Super Sportsman racers with his business Kramer Kraft. His cars were winning everywhere and were in high demand. In 1981, the Super Sportsman cars raced several times at Williams Grove Speedway, and all the races were won by a Kramer Kraft car. Also, at Silver Spring Speedway, Kramer Kraft cars were in Victory Lane some ten times during the 1982 season.

The Super Sportsman class has been a steppingstone class for many years, used by drivers to gain valuable time and experience before moving on to the faster Sprint Cars. Kramer loved to work on and build them, perhaps because his own career was started in the Super Sportsman class. The winged Super Sportsman Sprint Cars did not look much different from a regular Sprint Car; however, Kramer tells the differences in his own words:

> The thing that most people don't know is the difference between a Super Sportsman and a Sprinter. Basically, they both look alike in appearance. The

difference between a Sportsman and a Sprint Car is that on a Sportsman car you must have a 90-inch wheelbase to start off. The next thing is that there must be a box frame on the bottom of the chassis that is 58 inches long. Then you have a clutch which is a triple disc clutch, that has a handle inside the roll cage that looks like a brake. This clutch disengages it into gear. There is a quick change rear in them, but no open tube rear like in the Sprints. They have an axle housing. Another thing is that there cannot be any offset at all. The motor must sit in the center of the wheelbase. The roll cage must be 30 inches wide from the shoulder height, and to where it's welded on top of the box frame. There is no frame width. You also can't have power steering in the car. The only other thing I can think of is that the motor must not be over the 350 cubic inch limit. One thing is for sure, a Super Sportsman car is definitely harder to build than a Sprint. There are more pieces to be made, and the rules at the track they run on, carry a stricter involvement.

Listening to Kramer spouting off the rules as if they were written down, one must remember that all this information was just from his memory.

Truly a master at his craft, Kramer also described how he builds a car from scratch:

The first thing that I do is draw it out to scale on the table. Then once I have that done, I tack pieces to the frame table. Instead of making a jig up, I just change the table. Once that's done, I start making the frame pieces. I make the right side then I make the left side. The sides are most of the time welded together. Then what I do is tear down the table and stand the side rails upright. I then put the roll cage on, and then consider the width of the car from front to back. The frame is tapered, as I measure everything. I then go ahead and place the motor in, so it can be altered and centered. Then it's time to put in the crosspieces of the frame and the diagonals in the roll cage. What you should have now is a complete frame sitting there spot-welded. The rear of the frame would measure 30 inches wide and would be tapered to the front to 21 inches. It makes the frame much stronger.

I would then tear the frame apart and basically weld it with the main components on, like the rear, and what have you. When I start welding the frame completely, I make sure it doesn't twist, as it is a very important thing to watch. After the entire frame is welded up, then I start adding torsion arms front and rear, and other components including the bird cage. If the frame looks ready to be put on wheels, then now is the time. Then the extra pieces are put on such as the throttle linkage, brake pedal, side rails, full tank mounts [fuel tank] and bumpers.

As I near completion of the Super Sportsman chassis, I go over it with a fine tooth comb before the hood and side panels are placed on the car. Then after that the next thing is to put on the wing mounts and the wing itself, before the final thing to do is to have it painted and lettered.

Kramer Kraft cars' craftsmanship was second to none. Kramer only used the best aircraft-certified tubing for his chassis. The best materials, coupled with a streamlined design refined over the years by the master himself, produced a bare chassis weighing only one hundred and ninety pounds. Despite the frame's light weight, safety was always a priority for Kramer, and he used his own experiences to make his Kramer Kraft cars safer for everyone.

> The safety feature of the car is very important. Each time I build a chassis, I try to come up with something else on the part of safety. The one thing I really worry about is the roll cage. As far as I'm concerned, the cage is what saves lives. I build cars so that if anything comes off in a crash, it's the front or rear of the frame before that cage would go. Don't get me wrong, I don't build cars so that they fall apart. At the speeds that these cars are going today, anything can happen, as it all depends how and what angle it takes the worst beating. I have a new style roll cage now where it's all one piece from the top frame rail all the way down to the box frame. It is much easier to work on and a lot easier to weld.
>
> Another thing I did for safety was to weld the seat in instead of dzus buttoning it in the car. I weld the tabs and bolt the seat in. This past summer I had a crash in a Sprint and the seat busted. After that, I knew what I would be putting in any car that is a Kramer Kraft. The other safety thing is that I don't skimp on any bracing on the roll cage. Again, that roll cage is very important. I have a lot of pride in the work I do, and I have a guy named Ed Grimsey who is my right-hand man, who also has the same respect for building a chassis. It might take me a lot of time to construct a chassis, but I do it with a lot of things on my mind, such as safety and good neat work.

With Kramer's forward thinking about safety and a proven winning record, Kramer Kraft chassis were in high demand in the early 1980s. The price range for a complete Kramer Kraft rolling chassis ranged from $11,000 to $12,000 in 1983, a far cry from what Kramer's first Super Sportsman racer cost in 1969. While the price of racing continued to increase, making it harder for teams to compete in all forms of racing during the early 1980s, one side benefit was that the cars were indeed much safer than they had been just a few years before, and they continued to gain safety features as racing progressed through the decade.

While Kramer loved to drive, he was equally happy building cars in his shop. To this day, photos of Fred Putney, Larry Jackson, Paul Miller, Rich Eichelberger and Gary Wolford adorn the wall, all taking checkered flags in Kramer Kraft cars. Kramer said one time, "Everybody I have built cars for have been real good people. They let me build it the way I want to. I build a car as if I'm going to run it myself. I have put a lot of ideas in those chassis." The friendships made and races won made Kramer Kraft a successful business that would carry on for many more years and would help support not only Kramer's racing, but his family as well.

Kramer would get the call to race at the famed Knoxville Speedway in the Knoxville Nationals for Bob Trostle in 1983. With over one hundred Sprint Cars trying to make the twenty-two-car A-Main feature event, just making the race could make or break one's racing year. Driving the #20 Bob Trostle Racing house car, Kramer found himself solidly qualifying for the main event in the nineteenth position in his first attempt at the race. Driving Trostle's coilover car, Kramer would move up nicely during the running of the thirty-lap event to finish in the twelfth position in his first A-Main Knoxville National race. Car owner Bob Trostle, who had won the Knoxville Nationals twice before, once

Two legends of the sport teamed up at the 1983 Knoxville Nationals. Bob Trostle (left) and Kramer (right) pose beside the #20. In his first running at the Nationals, Kramer qualified for the A-main and ended up finishing a solid twelfth.

in 1977 with Doug Wolfgang driving and once in 1980 with Steve Kinser, was happy to have yet another one of his Sprint Cars finish well in what many consider to be the biggest race of the year. Kramer would run more races for Trostle at Knoxville and at Greg Weld's I-70 Speedway, where Kramer was in contention for the win until a parts failure knocked him out of the race.

The pair would end the year running again the "Moody Mile" at the New York State fairgrounds in Syracuse, New York. The track's nickname, the "Moody Mile," was given in 1970 when Wesley Moody became the first driver to average one hundred miles per hour for one lap around the track. The large one-mile track was not for the faint of heart, with drivers reaching speeds not normally seen on the half-mile and smaller ovals. Car owner Bob Trostle was pleased with Kramer's twenty-fourth-place finish in the A-Main feature event, but what Trostle remembered most about the weekend was having "dippy eggs" for breakfast. The Midwestern-based Trostle got quite a kick over the term "dippy eggs" (over easy fried eggs), which was used commonly by those living in and around central Pennsylvania.

There is no doubt that Kramer and Trostle thought highly of each other and had much respect for each other's talents, so it was no surprise that at the end of the 1983 season, Bob Trostle asked Kramer to drive for him in Australia and represent the United States of America in the land down under. In some ways, Kramer and Bob Trostle were very much alike in their passion for Sprint Car racing. Doug Wolfgang remembers Kramer's lifestyle well:

> For one thing, Kramer lived Sprint Cars. He lived, ate and breathed it every day. In the wintertime, he went out to his garage and worked on race cars. He built them and he repaired them for different customers so even on his off days, he was still around a car or doing something to a race car every single day. I think I am kind of the same way now that I don't race anymore and I still have a race shop. I think I am smarter now than I ever was when I drove during the peak of my career. I am around these cars day in and day out and you hear ten different stories every day about racing and you keep that in your mind. If I had the exuberance and the athletic talent I had when I drove, along with some of the smarts I obtained later in life, I think I would have been even faster when I was racing. You know, most guys that race work a job, or they race for money until they can't make enough, then they go get a job somewhere to support their racing. Then for eight or ten hours a day they are not around racing. Then all of a sudden they get tired of racing on the weekends because they can't make any more money or they

get too old. So they stop going to the races and they are not around it they lose the capacity to learn and to keep in touch with everything. But Kramer was not that way. Even when I drove for Weikert in the 1980s, he did not necessarily drive the unlimited Sprint Cars in central Pennsylvania anymore on a full-time basis, but he could afford to race the URC at that time. So I did not get to see Kramer race very much the four years I was in central Pennsylvania, but every week it seemed like he would win a race somewhere. He would run the URC or for different guys in the local area. He would come back and race the Grove every now and then on a pick-up ride. But he was always a competitor and a threat to win even in a car that was not dead-on first class. So that always told me that he knew what was going on and how to make a car work. He was a sharp driver and the URC was no walk in the park. There were a lot of good drivers in that series. He also built his own stuff, which just adds to your ability as a driver. There's not a lot of guys that know if you move the motor forward or back a half inch what it really does, or if you move the torsion tubes up or down or the shock mounts up or down, how that makes the car different. Kramer knew that because he built his own stuff and if it did not work he would work on it until he got it the way he wanted it to drive. That gave him a huge leg up on his competitors, especially when he raced in the URC, because most of those guys were weekend racers, and let's face it, we are all weekend racers except for a few World of Outlaw Sprint Car guys. So they all have to go to a job through the week and make a living and Kramer's job was working on cars so he was around it every day, all day, and I think that helped him. That is what gave him the drive to continue to it.

Before leaving for the long flight across the sea to tackle the best Australia had to offer, Kramer slipped back into a USAC car at the Hoosier 100 at the Indiana State Fairgrounds. Kramer was asked by car owner Lloyd Stevens to run his #21 Ofixco USAC Silver Crown car after neither of his drivers, Ron Shuman and Jerry Stone, could make the race because they were contending for the points in other series. The car, which was Pancho Carter's last dirt track car, was a quality ride, so Kramer said, "I'd give it a try and see how it went." It went well: After starting eighteenth on a track that had a single groove, Kramer was able to work himself up all the way to a fourth-place finish. Kramer had what many considered to be the fastest car on the track, but simply ran out of laps before he could challenge for any more positions. The race was won by Chuck Gurney leading by fifteen seconds over second-place Sheldon Kinser.

With little time to rest after the racing season, Kramer, Rocky Hodges and Bob Trostle got right to disassembling their Sprint Cars in order for them to be shipped to Australia. The culmination of a two-year

Shown here at the 1983 Hoosier 100, Kramer finished fourth in the #21 Ofixco car owned by Lloyd Stevens.

effort by owner and chassis builder Bob Trostle and Australian Speedway promoter Con Migro, it took an enormous amount of effort to get both the drivers and cars to the land down under. The American contingent would ship the disassembled cars by boat to Australia and then reassemble them there before racing. Following the eight-race series, five races at Claremont Speedway and three races at Bunbury Speedway, the cars would then be sold to various racers in Australia.

Migro remembers the effort to get the Americans to come over and race: "I don't think the public realized the work that goes into getting the top competitors to race here. There are the flights and accommodations to arrange, quarantine and customs, transport while they are here and a host of other small things." Kramer would also gain a new nickname during his time in Australia. While everyone in America came to know Kramer as "the Pink Panther," those down under would know him as "Krafty" Kramer Williamson. Kramer drove a beautiful red, white and blue Bob Trostle Sprint Car. The #37 car was adorned with a huge USA on the top wing and had a star-spangled front wing. On the hood of the patriotic machine were the words in blue and red,

"Krafty" Kramer Williamson. The Americans' coming to race in Australia was somewhat similar to when the World of Outlaws would come to Pennsylvania to race the "PA Posse." The local Australians wanted to show the Americans this was their turf and they had the top cars and drivers, just like the local boys in Pennsylvania wanted to show they could hold their own against the Outlaws back in the States. The friendly rivalry was always well attended by fans and hotly contested by the competitors on the tight, narrow tracks of Australia. The tour was a success for everyone involved. The fans got to see the best Sprint Car drivers Australia and America had to offer for eight great races. The Americans had a great showing in the land down under as both Hodges and Williamson brought home multiple victories in feature events during the tour, with Kramer winning two races. Because of the overall success of the whole tour, Kramer would head back to Australia

Bob Trostle assembled drivers Rocky Hodges and Kramer Williamson to race in Australia during the winter in 1984. Here, Kramer stands in front of his patriotic Team USA Sprint Car.

Kramer races to victory at Claremont Speedway in Australia. His trademark smooth style won over many fans and earned him two wins during the tour.

three more times over his career to race the country's best and represent America. Heading back to the States with two wins in his pocket, a happy Kramer used the rest of the winter to concentrate on his Kramer Kraft business and get ready for the fast-approaching 1984 race season.

Kramer's close relationship with Bob Trostle helped lead car owner Joe Fiore to seek out Kramer to drive his #8 United Racing Club (URC) Sprint Car in 1983. Kramer drove the immaculate #8 Sprint Car part-time in 1983, winning one race. The success of that year would lead to a fourteen-race schedule for Fiore in 1984. Kramer remembered that period and the connection with Fiore:

> The early '80s were lean years. I don't know why. I didn't really have anything to run. How I got hooked up with Joe Fiore was in '83; I had gone to Australia with Bob Trostle. Fiore bought Trostle cars. One day, Trostle mentioned to Fiore about giving me a call. Joe didn't want to run all of the shows, just some. We won something like seven out of fourteen races.

Kramer's year would consist of running the #8 Fiore Sprint Car in the traveling URC series, running the Ofixco USAC car in select events, and running his own #73 Sprint Car at various Sprint Car shows, including the World of Outlaws. On June 2, 1984, Kramer gave owner Joe Fiore his first win of the year at Winchester Speedway, located in Winchester, Virginia. Kramer beat out twenty-eight cars that night to win in what many consider to be the most competitive time in URC history. During the early eighties, drivers like Dave Kelly, Don Kreitz, Buck Buckley, Glenn Fitzcharles and Fran Hogue all ran the URC on a regular basis and were contenders in the URC Championship. The URC regulars, along with invaders (drivers who would come race the URC on a limited basis) like Fred Rahmer, Bobby Wilkins and others, made the URC series one of the most competitive and hardest to win in the country. The race at Winchester Speedway was the first at the track for the URC Sprint Cars in twenty years. Kramer started in the fifteenth position and thrilled the record crowd by passing a car per lap, including Dave Kelly, a five-time feature winner already that year. Once Kramer worked himself into the first-place position, he easily cruised to his first win of many during the 1984 season. The well-earned win helped to ease the pain of some early season mechanical failures that plagued the team's efforts.

The team would not have to wait long for the next win as Kramer again put the #8 Fiore Sprinter at the front of the pack at Bridgeport Speedway on June 9, 1984. Again, it was Kramer and Dave Kelly who had a tough fight for the victory. Kelly, the previous week's winner at Hagerstown Speedway, and Kramer had now finished one and two for the last three races and were providing fans with some of the best racing they had seen in years.

Kramer's family was super-proud of his performances and even took out an ad in the local paper for Father's Day to congratulate him on his win. The ad read, "Congratulations Kramer Williamson on your feature win at Bridgeport Raceway in the Fiore Sprinter. P.S. Happy Father's Day Daddy! Love Kurtis." As always, racing continued to be a family affair, with his wife Sharon and young son Kurtis supporting Kramer's racing and winning in every way possible.

Indeed, Kramer was on a roll, and the momentum of first-place finishes continued in the very next race at Big Diamond Speedway. The red-hot Kramer Williamson raced past all his competitors yet again to

Driving the Joe Fiore #8, Kramer won seven URC feature events during the 1984 season including the Joe Fiore, Sr., memorial race at Bridgeport Speedway.

claim his third victory in four races and his second race win in a row. With thirty-seven cars on hand for the race, Kramer bested them all, with Fred Rahmer finishing second.

Kramer would take a break from the URC action to debut his own #73 Kramer Kraft Sprint Car at Susquehanna Speedway on July 1, 1984. The car, along with Kramer and his family, almost didn't make it to the track. On the way to the track, an axle broke on the trailer, sending the trailer and tow rig sideways on the Interstate. After recovering from the excitement of the incident, the team managed to make it to the track just in time to qualify for the feature race. Debuting what many considered to be one of the most beautiful Sprint Cars Kramer ever drove, the pink pearl colored Sprinter was expertly lettered by Kramer's brother George Williamson. The beautiful car featured numbers that were twenty-four karat white gold and hand-laid stripes that accented the colors perfectly. While the car was beautiful, it was also fast. Although running late because of the trailer axle failure and not being able to shake down the car completely, Kramer finished second to Keith Kauffman in the feature event.

While many fans continue to talk about what many considered to be the best-looking Sprint Car in the East, Kramer jumped back into his URC Fiore #8 and continued his winning ways. Kramer took the Gambler chassis #8 Sprinter to the front in dominating fashion at Grandview Speedway, winning his fourth URC Sprint Car race of the year.

Although Kramer was thick into the race season, he always found time to say "Thanks" and show his appreciation to those who supported them even if they literally lived halfway around the world. Printed in the Claremont Speedway Track program in 1984 was a letter from Kramer to Con Migro thanking him and his fans for their hospitality during his visit to Australia. The program read:

> Dear Mr. Migro
> Just wanted to drop you a line to say "Thanks" for your great hospitality during my recent visit to your country. I really enjoyed my visit and I think your people are the warmest, friendliest people I have ever met. I wish my racing could have been more competitive. Hopefully, I will get another chance to come over to your country and put on a good racing show for your fans. Please tell your racing fans "Thanks" for their support of what I feel is the greatest sporting event ever.... SPRINT CAR RACING. I only wish the American people supported the sport as the Australian racing fans do. Their warm, friendly welcome gave me a great deal of respect for Australia. Thanks again for a great time and a great racing experience, one that I will always treasure. Thank you Con Migro for giving me the opportunity to come to your country and race.
> Sincerely,
> Kramer Williamson

Interactions like this were common throughout Kramer's career and are reflective of the kind of person he was. It is no wonder he was not only a fan favorite in Australia, but also a favorite right here at home as well. Many a fan has been on the receiving end of Kramer's kindness and generosity over the years, which has earned him a large fanatic fan base. That fan base would show up to the second URC show at Grandview Speedway on July 22 when Kramer yet again would earn the victory in the Fiore #8 car. The win was Kramer's fifth of the year in the URC division.

Kramer would take a small break from URC action in August to concentrate his efforts once again at making the field for the annual running of the Knoxville Nationals in Knoxville, Iowa. Kramer again would drive for his friend Bob Trostle in the #20 Sprint Car. The car would be the same Vise-Grip–sponsored Sprinter that Steve Kinser drove during his first win at Knoxville in 1980. For the second year in a row, with over a hundred Sprint Cars just trying to make the field, Kramer would make the A-Main feature event. Not bad at all to qualify in a five-year-old used race car that he had never driven before against the country's premier racing talent. Kramer finished in twenty-first position with wife Sharon and son Kurtis looking on. While hoping for a better result, Kramer was still happy just to make the A-Main in such a prestigious race. In a show of sportsmanship, one of Kramer's former owners, Bob Weikert, donated two tires to Kramer on race day. To show his appreciation, Kramer took out an ad in the newspaper that read, "Thank You! Bob Weikert for the two tires at Knoxville. I really appreciated it. Kramer Williamson."

Kramer returned home to Pennsylvania to finish third at Selinsgrove Speedway driving the #8 Fiore Sprinter in a URC race, as well as finishing second in his own #73 Sprint Car at Selinsgrove Speedway to Doug Wolfgang in the #29 Weikert Livestock car. Even though Kramer and Doug Wolfgang were competitors on the track, Doug remembers Kramer's hospitality during the early to mid–'80s:

> When I came out to Pennsylvania to drive the #29 Weikerts Livestock car, the mechanic on that car was Davey Brown, Sr., and Davey Brown, Jr. Davey Jr. was married to Debbie, who was Sharon Williamson's sister, and all the sisters worked at Williams Grove, Sharon, Debbie and Sandy. I got to know their family really well. I really liked Debbie because she did not care I was a race driver and just liked me for being me. Because of that, I liked her and her family a lot. She got along great with my wife Jeri and everything. Even though we would come in and live there for like nine months out of the year, we were still treated somewhat as outsiders because we still lived in South Dakota and our kids still went to school out there and everything. But Davey Brown, Kramer and their wives and a few others sure made us feel welcome and at home. Even though you're a racer and racing is a big community you still only know a few people to call friends. I guess I could compare it to the NBA. There are a million basketball players, but there are only a few hundred NBA players, so when you compare that to the level of unlimited Sprint Cars in the 1980s, there was a lot of racers, but you know all the top racers and are only close with a few of them. At that point in time (mid–'80s), I was winning races much like Kramer had done in that

area in the mid–1970s. So I became one of the superstars in that area. When you race probably seventy percent of your schedule within three to four hours of Williams Grove Speedway, I was still somewhat of an outsider due to the fact I was from South Dakota. But Sharon and Debbie (Sharon's sister, who was married to Davey Brown) made me feel right at home when I was around them, and Kramer as well. He was always giving me crap and I loved that. I could win fifteen races in a row and still was not crap to him. I used to get a kick out of that.

Before Kramer could win his sixth race of the year for the Fiore team, Joe Fiore, Sr., would pass away at the age of sixty-seven. The patriarch of the family lost a long and courageous battle with cancer. Though he had never raced himself, he first fielded a race car in 1933. Always known for immaculately kept and prepared machines, Fiore was devoted to the URC and loved the competition of the club. Although Joe Fiore, Sr., had given the controls to his team to his son, Joe Jr., some fourteen years earlier, he was still very much involved in the day-to-day operations of the team. The next race held after Fiore's passing was the twenty-five-lap event at Grandview. In a class act move, the track collected money from fans to award to the leader of lap #8 of the feature in honor of Joe Fiore, Sr. The race, which was also held as a memorial to Fiore, was hotly contested, but fate would prevail. Kramer Williamson, driving the Joe Fiore #8 Sprint Car, not only led lap #8, but won the race as well in dominating fashion, picking up his sixth win of the season and producing a fitting memorial to a racing legend.

The racing community would have yet another race to honor Joe Fiore, Sr., at Bridgeport Raceway on September 8, 1984. Kramer and Don Kreitz, Jr., waged an all-out battle for the victory with Kramer coming out on top to honor his late car owner Joe Fiore, Sr. Joe McMahon and former URC president Louis Kunz presented the special memorial trophy to Kramer in Victory Lane as Kramer celebrated his seventh victory with wife Sharon and son Kurtis joining him for the special moment. Kramer ended the 1984 URC season with seven wins and finished in seventh place in the URC points championship, an amazing feat when you consider he only competed in approximately half the URC races that season.

Although the URC Sprint Cars would not fire up again until the following year, there were a couple more events on the central Pennsylvania calendar that Kramer had his eyes on: the Williams Grove Speedway National Open and the season-ending World of Outlaws show at

Selinsgrove Speedway. Kramer drove his own Kramer Kraft car that he built from scratch in both events. Kramer finished in the seventh position at the Williams Grove Speedway National Open as his friend and competitor Doug Wolfgang won the feature event in a tight battle with Steve Smith. The season-ending race at Selinsgrove Speedway is the one that would have folks talking throughout the winter about what they saw on the track.

Kramer would test himself and his Kramer Kraft car against the World of Outlaws for the season-ending race on October 7, 1984. The capacity crowd was treated to a four-way battle between Kramer, Doug Wolfgang, Steve Kinser and Brian Seidel. Everyone brought his A game to the last race and it was evident even in the qualifying heats. The ten-lap track record was broken three different times during the night's qualifiers, first by Dave Wickham, then by Kramer and finally by Jim Nace, who set the ten-lap record at 3:10.76. At the start of the thirty-lap event, Kramer leaped to the lead in what some of the area papers touted as "the best race in the history of the speedway." While Kramer was running the top up front, both Steve Kinser and Doug Wolfgang were making their moves to get into contention for the win. Late in the race, Kinser tried the low line to pass the cushion riding Kramer, but each time they came off the corner, Kramer would have just enough momentum to keep the lead. The race for first and second allowed Doug Wolfgang to get in the mix as he started to shove his nose into the battle as well. On the twenty-ninth lap Kinser made a low, sweeping move off turn four and passed Kramer for good, leaving Kramer to defend against a hard-charging Doug Wolfgang. At the finish, it would be Kinser, Kramer and Wolfgang in the top three. During the Victory Lane interview, Steve Kinser said, "This is the hardest I've had to race all year. I've raced Williamson and Wolfgang before and I trusted them enough to stick it tight with the two of them." A heartfelt compliment from a driver who became the "King of the Outlaws" and the standard of competitiveness in Sprint Car racing today.

In *Flat Out* magazine in 2000, Kramer remembered the sting of losing that race: "I nearly beat Kinser that night. I was running my own deal and didn't have a lot of money. We didn't have enough money for a new right rear tire so I ran an old one. I led twenty-nine of thirty laps until the tire went away and Kinser passed me." To this day, Kramer's wife, Sharon remembers a similar loss later in Kramer's career to Steve

Kinser for a completely different reason. "One of the prizes for winning the race that night at Selinsgrove was a Cabbage Patch Doll. It was right at the time when everyone wanted one and it was impossible to find them in the stores anywhere and people were getting a ridiculous price for them. I wanted one to give my daughter Felecia. All was good until we lost the race on the last lap. It was the only race I was mad Kramer didn't win and I can still remember it like it was yesterday."

While waiting for the 1985 racing season, the Kramer Kraft shop was in full in swing building chassis of all kinds. Stepping out from the umbrella of building Sprint Car chassis, Kramer ventured into building an Oswego Super Modified chassis for Dean Hoag. Of course, he still had a list of drivers who wanted their own Kramer Kraft Sprint Car chassis, like rookie driver Donnie Beaver, who was stepping up from

Kramer gave his old friend Bob Trostle a call in the mid-eighties and ordered Trostle chassis #431 to run in the Pennsylvania area.

120

the Super Sportsman class, and Silver Spring Sportsman drivers Howie Locke and Rich Eichelberger. "Kramer was always thinking of a way to make his cars faster," remembers former URC president John Zimmerman. "That's what he did. He would sit around all day and think about how to make the car faster. He would sit down there under his house and just stare at a chassis and you could just see the wheels turning." While the Kramer Kraft shop was keeping busy, Kramer got a call from Sprint Car owner Joe Harz to drive his #88 Carl Harz Furniture car and fill in for injured driver Meme DeSantis, who broke his arm in an auto accident. Of course, Kramer ran a limited schedule with the URC and Fiore #8 car again during the 1985 season as well. Lloyd Stephens also gave Kramer the opportunity to run six USAC races in his Ofixco #21 car, setting up a busy year of racing.

Kramer and the Fiore team started the URC season by entering the opening race at one of Kramer's favorite tracks, US 13 Speedway in Delmar, Delaware. Kramer started the season off on the right foot by putting the Fiore #8 Sprinter back in Victory Lane on April 15, 1985, beating Buck Buckley to the line for the win. Kramer followed up his early victory with a series of second-place finishes. He drove the #88 Joe Harz car to a hard-fought second-place finish at Selinsgrove Speedway, and the following week finished runner-up again in the URC series at Bridgeport Speedway behind first-time winner Tom Wanner. Always the gentleman racer, Kramer was quick to offer up congratulations even when he was the second-place finisher: "He did a good job, he really did. You can't take anything from his win as he beat a lot of good cars. I'll tell you, I couldn't catch him at all." A compliment like that from Kramer went a long way with his competitors. Fellow URC driver Ed Aiken told the *Patriot-News* in an interview that Kramer "wasn't just an awesome racer, he was an awesome person. Guys like that are the reason you want to race ... to be like Kramer."

Kramer pulled double duty on May 18, 1985, at Lincoln Speedway when both the URC Sprints and Unlimited Sprint Cars of Central Pennsylvania invaded the track for a double-header. With a bad starting position in the URC feature, Kramer rocketed from seventeenth all the way to the fifth spot, passing the most cars of the event, but running out of laps to make it any further up the field. After his impressive charge in the #8 Fiore car, Kramer hopped back into the #88 Sprinter and again raced to a fourth-place finish in the night's thirty-lap feature. The

Always looking for edge, Kramer looks over one of his newly built Kramer Kraft chassis. Kramer's creations were successful in all classes of Sprint Car racing.

always adaptable Kramer ended his run in the #88 car at Selinsgrove Speedway a week later, finishing third before turning the wheel back over to a now fully healed Meme DeSantis.

Kramer's second and last URC victory of the year would again come at the same place he had won earlier in the year, US 13 Speedway in Delmar, Delaware. Kramer and Dave Kelly put on a fifteen-lap side-by-side duel that had fans on their feet. Kramer was handling well and running the low line while Kelly was in the high groove maintaining his momentum off the corners just enough to stay inches in front of Kramer. Coming off the fourth turn on the last lap, Kramer pulled ahead by mere inches to claim the victory and his second URC win of the year for the Fiore #8 team. The very next day, on June 6, 1985, at Grandview Speedway, the roles would be reversed, and it would be Dave Kelly who won the race, passing Kramer on the backstretch of the very last lap of the race. The good results came to an end in the URC division at Lincoln on July 3, 1985, when Kramer got tangled up in a wreck involving Fred Berger, Jr., and John Matrafailo. Flipping several times, Kramer emerged unhurt; however, the same could not be said for the beautiful #8 car, which was a total loss.

Kramer made a quick trip out to Oklahoma City to run his first race of the year driving the Ofixco USAC Silver Crown car. Kramer finished in third position behind leader Rick Hood and second-place Bob Ewell. It was another great result in the USAC series for Kramer. The ever-traveling driver would put racing on the back burner for a small while when he returned home to Pennsylvania, where his family would need him more than ever. Racing took a back seat to life in July of 1985 as Debbie Brown unexpectedly passed away from childbirth on July 25. Sharon and Debbie were pregnant together and were expecting their babies to grow up together. Debbie was the sister of Sharon Williamson and wife of mechanic Davey Brown. Debbie was loved by everyone who met her and worked the pit shack for Jack Gunn's KARS series and later became a scorer at Williams Grove Speedway. It was a huge loss for the Williamson family and everyone who knew Debbie. One of her biggest fans, Doug Wolfgang, for whom her husband was a mechanic at the time, remembers the dark days:

> When I heard about Debbie, I was devastated and I didn't want to go racing. When I found out about it, it took nine hours to do six hours' work on the car. I just wanted to pack the racing for the weekend in respect to Debbie.

Kramer built himself a new Kramer Kraft Sprint Car in 1985. The beautiful car was hand-lettered by his brother, George Williamson.

But Davey urged me to go to Eldora and to win the race for Debbie, and by God we did.

Doug Wolfgang was later asked by *Area Auto Racing News*, "What was your biggest win?" His response was easy:

The Kings Royal race at Eldora. The race sure paid ahead of the time, but I really didn't think about the money. I race the same for a thousand dollars or for a heat race as I do 15th. A race like Eldora made me prepare more at the shop. I get up on certain races. That race at Eldora meant a lot because Davey's wife died beforehand and we were not looking real good. Our whole team wasn't gelled together at the time as all our emotions were screwed up. The race was like a destiny, like it was going to happen no matter what. We shouldn't even have been able to get there [Eldora] because we really weren't ready to race. The car was prepared, but we weren't, due to Davey's wife passing away. We were emotionally messed up. It was quite satisfying for me to win that race. There wasn't a dry eye around.

124

At the end of Wolfgang's speech in Victory Lane, Doug simply said, "This one's for you, Debbie." It was a fitting tribute to a wonderful person who loved racing and made a friend out of everyone she met.

While Kramer and Sharon mourned the loss of their beloved family member, the racing community paid tribute in their own way, whether by dedicating a win in her memory or by an ad in the local racing paper. The racing community is a small family and when they lose one of their members, everyone feels the loss. As the mourning period passed, Kramer and his family found it hard, but went back to racing, although it was with heavy hearts.

The end of the season was at hand for the URC sprints. Kramer led the final race at Grandview before falling to a final finish of third in a hard-fought three-way battle with URC legends, winner Dave Kelly and runner-up Glenn Fitzcharles. Kramer ended the year with two URC wins and a fourteenth-place position in points, again running only part time in the series. It was one of the most successful years in the USAC series for Kramer, who ran six races in a quality car, the Stephens-owned #21 Ofixco Champ car. Kramer earned a fifteenth-place finish at Indianapolis Raceway Park in Indiana. This was his only asphalt race of the year in the Champ Car, and in Kramer's own words he was a little taken aback by the experience:

> Steve Stapp helped us out that night, but I just couldn't get used to keeping the car straight and burnt the tires right off. I don't know if they are the most fun things to drive. I compare them to the Modifieds around here, long wheelbases and slow reacting. I always like the car tight and I guess I grew up leaning on that wing.

Getting back on a surface he knew much better—dirt—Kramer started to have some good results as he got used to the slower-reacting Champ cars. He would post a third-place finish at Oklahoma City; an eleventh-place finish in Parkersburg, West Virginia; a fifth-place finish at Du Quoin, Illinois; a flat tire and a DNF at the Indiana State Fairgrounds; and at his last race in the USAC series for the year, he would end up seventh at Eldora Speedway in Ohio.

Still feeling the sting of losing their beloved Debbie earlier in the year, the Williamsons and extended family would finally have a reason for joyous celebration on September 9, 1985, when Kramer and Sharon Williamson welcomed a newborn daughter, Felecia Debra Williamson, into the world. The now family of four counted their blessings at the birth of Felecia and now had two kids to haul around to the races and enjoy life as a racing family. In typical racing family fashion, Felecia's arrival came on the heels of a night of racing at Susquehanna Speedway, as Sharon Williamson remembers:

> The night before Felecia was born we raced at Susquehanna Speedway. I remember climbing on top of the Jerry Stone Ofixco sprinter enclosed trailer to watch the race. I can't remember where Kramer finished that night but I do remember towing the Panther home on our open trailer that night. Kramer was still racey driving home and I told him to take it easy, not realizing my labor pains were going to be in a few short hours. I remember waking up and telling Kramer that I was in labor. He said to me, "Can we sleep another hour?" Let's just say he was lucky to race the rest of his career.
>
> We now had a problem of how to get to the hospital quickly. The clutch was out in my car and we could not drive it. You have to realize that my vehicle always came last for repairs, so with the clutch out of my car and his truck hooked up still to the trailer, the problem was how do we get to the hospital. Kurtis was staying overnight with my mom, so we ended up borrowing my sister's car to go to the hospital. We arrived at the hospital at 8:45 a.m. due to Harrisburg rush hour traffic and I had Felecia at 10:11 a.m. You might say we cut it a bit close.
>
> Kramer was running weekly shows for Frank Crash out in Ohio at the time. Kramer picked Felecia and myself up at the hospital on Wednesday morning when we were discharged, took us home, and him and his mom left for Sharon Speedway to race. Kramer made sure someone was there with us during his time away. My mom, Phyllis Beahm, stayed at my house until Kramer got back home.

Kramer stuck with the Fiore #8 team for the 1986 URC season. The black and white #8 Sprint Car was simply stunning to view. It was the first year that the Fiore team ran the black and white color scheme, as they usually painted their cars red and white. The Bob Trostle chassis car was not only beautiful, but fast as well, taking Kramer to a second-place finish at Selinsgrove Speedway behind Frankie Kerr during the early season opener. Kramer's only win of the 1986 season came at Hagerstown Speedway in the #8 on June 13, with Sharon, Kurtis and Felecia by his side. From the thirteenth starting position, Kramer meticulously worked his way through the field until on lap seventeen he grabbed the lead from Brian Seidel and never looked back.

The win was Kramer's sole victory for 1986. He put on some amazing shows of driving talent and had many close encounters with winning again, but for one reason or the other just could not close the deal.

At US 13 in July, he wowed the crowd by coming from the last starting position to eighth in just a few laps and appeared to be headed to the front before breaking and coming to a stop on the speedway. It was a sign of things to come for Kramer. He would run both the Momorella #57 USAC car and the #15 Beletsky USAC cars in 1986, but both would break while running strong, resulting in two DNFs.

Now a seasoned racer, Kramer had been through lean times, before but no one expected it would be four and a half years before he would win his next race. Kramer continued to race including another trip across the ocean to Australia to race Sprint Cars with Bob Trostle. On his 1986 trip across the ocean, he was joined by a young boy who was said to be a driving phenomenon. His name was Jeff Gordon, the same Jeff Gordon who became one of NASCAR's greatest champions and drivers.

Kramer's victory on June 13, 1986, at Hagerstown Speedway was the first time that all four family members appeared together in Victory Lane. From left to right: Kramer, Kurtis, Sharon and Felecia Williamson.

Despite what some think, Kramer never took a year off from 1986 to 1991. He picked up rides here and there as well as running his own #73 Pink Panther car during that time, but could just never find the success he was accustomed to earlier in his career. In his own words, "We really struggled. Dale helped me build a car I ran in '86 and a while after that. We didn't have a fiberglass hood. George and I built our hood from aluminum. I remember welding it." Kramer even gave his old friend Bob Trostle a call to try out one of his chassis to see if it would change Kramer's luck. Trostle delivered chassis #431 to Kramer in December of 1989. Although Kramer put in some good performances, he was unable to break out of the rut and get back into Victory Lane. It was a changing time for Sprint Car racing; escalating costs made getting a quality ride even more challenging than ever.

For Kramer, the top rides in Pennsylvania had simply dried up. Some had merely written Kramer off as a "has-been" or as too old to be competitive and were putting young up-and-coming drivers in their cars. Kramer, in reality, was not that old in 1991. He was 41 and was forced to run his own car during much of those lean times. As Kramer often said, "I am not old, I just started young." Not having the funding and big sponsors no doubt contributed to the lean years of the late 1980s. Kramer continued to keep himself busy in his first-floor shop, building and repairing cars until 1991, when a phone call would jump-start his career and launch one of the most talked-about comebacks in Sprint Car history.

7

Resurgence

When most people talk about Kramer Williamson and his career in racing, the conversation will turn to which part of his career is being talked about. The first half of Kramer's career from 1969 to 1990 is considered by many to be the first chapter in his long racing career. Many considered chapter two in his career to be his time with the URC from 1991 to 2013. While the first half of his career was worthy enough for most to get into the Sprint Car Hall of Fame, Kramer was about to add to his résumé in a way few saw coming.

It all started with a phone call in 1991 from car owner Henry Fenimore. Fenimore, from New Castle, Delaware, was a successful car owner who fielded the bright yellow B&F Towing–sponsored #28F Sprint Car. Fenimore was all set for an all-out assault for the URC Championship and had locked down the five-time champion and URC's second-winningest driver, Dave Kelly, to drive his car for the 1991 season. The day before the opening event at US 13 Speedway in Delmar, Delaware, Fenimore got a call from Dave Kelly around lunchtime saying he was sorry, but he would be unable to drive for Fenimore because he had secured another Sprint Car ride in central Pennsylvania.

That Friday, Fenimore gave Kramer a call and left a message on his answering machine to call him back as soon as possible. Fenimore and Kramer knew each other through Fenimore's brother, Bobby. Bobby Fenimore, like his brother, fielded race cars as well, but in the Modified division. Henry had tried once before to get Kramer to drive one of his Sprint Cars, but Kramer could not accept due to his previous commitments with other rides in the local central Pennsylvania circuit. Fenimore remembers Kramer's return call: "At three-thirty, he called me back and said he'd drive the car, just for the first two shows. His car was wrecked, so he was free for the weekend. I've known Kramer for

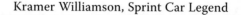

From the beginning, racing has always been a family affair for the William-son family. In Victory Lane, Kramer stands with his son Kurtis and daughter Felecia.

a long time, so I had no problem asking him to drive. He's a sportsman, not mouthy, and a heck of a driver."

Kramer drove the Buckley chassis Sprint Car at the season opener like a man possessed. He easily won his heat, starting from the seventh position and passing some very fast cars on his way to the lead. In the feature, he drew the twelfth starting spot, and on lap three of the twenty-five-lap event, he rocketed into the lead. Dealing with lapped traffic became an issue, but Kramer had a comfortable enough lead and made good use of his track position to secure the win in his first time out with the #28F team. It was all smiles in Victory Lane as Kramer pulled the bright yellow Fenimore car in for a celebration. The forty-one-year-old Sprint Car legend made his second and supposedly last start for Fenimore on Sunday at Bridgeport Speedway in New Jersey and waged a war with fellow URC legend Glenn Fitzcharles. Bob Swavely won the race, but every eye in the place was focused on Kramer and Fitzcharles battling for fourth spot. The crowd was on its feet as the two swapped positions before the fall of the checkered flag. Kramer beat Fitzcharles to the line in a classic display of driving ability by both drivers.

Kramer's temporary weekend seat in the Fenimore #28F was indeed a success, and the task of finding a full-time driver for the rest of the season was on. Fenimore planned to call a few drivers during the week before the next weekend's events, but the word was already out that one of the top URC Sprint Car rides was looking for a driver. Fenimore's phone rang constantly for the first two days after Kramer's successful week, with drivers from all over the East Coast wanting a shot at driving his car for the season. In all, twenty-seven drivers called to show interest in piloting the #28F. In an interview with *Flat Out* magazine in 2000, Fenimore remembered the situation that week and why he wanted Kramer as his full-time guy:

> Kramer was my first choice as a replacement for Dave. At first, he agreed only to race that weekend. He started twelfth and won the first time he ever ran the car. When we got home, we had a lot of drivers interested in the ride, including Billy Pauch. When I told 'em Kramer had agreed to stay the year, some felt we were making a mistake. I knew better. I judged Kramer on what he did in the past, not what he was doing at the time, trying to run his car out of his own pocket. His win that first night wasn't a fluke. What he brought to the team was, first of all, talent, and then a great knowledge of racing and setups. He was able to click very well with others on the team. He is a great sportsman and represents the sponsors well. Away from the track, he is a party animal. He can light up a room. He's great to have around when things aren't going good because he can change people's attitude.

Indeed, Kramer decided to stay with Fenimore through the season and focused on winning a URC Championship for the car owner. Winning the championship was the main focus for Fenimore's 1991 season and the addition of Kramer's driving full-time just put his goals back on the right track. Fenimore was no stranger to successful race seasons. Fenimore and his brothers, Herb and Bob, were all successful car owners in several different divisions. Running under the aegis of the family's business, B&F Towing, driver Rich Pratt was super-successful in the Modified division.

While brothers Herb and Bob concentrated on the Modified division, Henry's heart was with the Sprint Cars. His roots in racing were

In his years driving the #28 car for owner Henry Fenimore, Kramer won back-to-back URC Championships in 1991 and 1992.

based in the Micro Midget racing at Delaware's Airport Speedway, where he won over seventy feature wins and five championships in his role as car owner. The well-respected Fenimore also served as president of the Blackbird Micro Midget Race Club and helped elevate both the club and Airport Speedway into one of the most well-known and premier Micro Midget tracks in the U.S. today. In 1989, Fenimore jumped up to the URC sprints and had some success with driver Gary Gollub, who gave him his first taste of victory in 1989 and gave him three more wins in 1990. With all the skills of a seasoned businessman and much experience in the racing industry, Fenimore was one of the most well-rounded car owners in the URC, making him a perfect owner for a seasoned driver like Kramer.

If the team needed a sign that they made the right decision hiring Kramer as their driver, they would not have to wait long. In the third race of the year and first race since sealing the yearlong deal, the URC headed back to Delaware International Speedway. Kramer would silence the critics and win yet again in only his third time driving the Fenimore #28F Sprint Car. This time starting from the eighth position, Kramer mesmerized the Delaware crowd as he picked off his competitors and won his second feature race of the year. The super-consistent Kramer posted top-ten finishes at Grandview and Fonda Speedways before again returning to Victory Lane at Bridgeport Speedway, where he split the night's twin twelve-lap features. It was a history-making night in more ways than one. Fellow URC driver Mares Stellfox became the first female in URC history to win a URC qualifying race, paving the way for more female drivers in URC's future. Also, two URC legends would share Victory Lane. URC's all-time race winner and four-time URC Champion Glenn Fitzcharles would win one of the twelve-lap events, splitting the evening's features with Kramer Williamson, who had yet to win any of his championships with the URC. It was a symbolic changing-of-the-guard moment as Fitzcharles was at the end of his long record-breaking URC career and Kramer was just in his first full season of URC competition.

In fact, at the very next URC event at Selinsgrove Speedway, Fitzcharles won his seventieth URC Sprint Car race. Kramer finished a solid third in the race after doing double duty for the night racing his central Pennsylvania Sprint Car. Kramer flipped his #73 Sprint Car in practice, making his third-place finish in the #28F URC Sprinter all the more impressive. Kramer did run his #73 self-owned Sprint Car in some of the central Pennsylvania shows with help from a man named Bill Burkhardt. Burkhardt would sponsor Kramer's pink #73 and drive all the way from Maine to watch him race. Also, Frank Campbell helped with the cost of tires and spare parts here and there, and of course, as always, Kramer's parents still helped as much as they could with defraying the enormous cost of running a big-block Sprint Car in Pennsylvania. The cost had simply outgrown what Kramer could afford on his own, and the limited rules of the URC club, coupled with an owner taking care of the bills, made it a no-brainer to concentrate his efforts on the URC Sprint Cars.

Many other organizations looked down at the limited Sprints of the URC, but Kramer and many others felt quite different about racing the URC Sprints. In an interview with Cher Zimmerman in 1991 at Delaware, Kramer explained why:

> Many people from other Sprint organizations think of the URC as second-rate. I'll tell you right now, it's not. When you're running limited tires, motors, and wings, you have to be sharp. I live a half hour from Williams Grove and ten minutes from Susquehanna. Port Royal, Selinsgrove, and Lincoln are less than an hour from my home. Why am I driving nine hours to Canada, seven hours to Weedsport and three hours to Delaware? Because it's something different and challenging. It's not like you have a certain setup for each track. For example, last time I was here at Delaware, the track was dry and slick. Tonight, I got fooled because it was so tacky.

A few mechanicals kept Kramer out of Victory Lane for the next few races. He was well on his way to yet another victory at the June 29 race at Delaware International when a radius rod broke, ending his chances at winning three in a row at the Delaware half-mile oval. By mid-season, the points battle for the URC Championship was a two-way deadlock between Kramer and Billy Ellis. Kramer remembers the attitude the team had towards the points race during the mid-year stretch:

> When Henry hired me, winning the title was one of his goals. I know one of the reasons why we accomplished that goal was because Henry put no pressure on me. He knows I run as hard as I can, as long as I can. I'm not the type of driver who looks ahead far enough to win a championship. The point lead at one time was less than ten points. We decided, after discussing it, that we would put the points out of our heads. If the car ran fast, the points would come along. I told Henry that the wheels could come off the car before I'd pull it in.

Kramer would pull out a small lead in the points after surviving and winning a crash-filled race at Albany Saratoga Speedway in New York. Kramer and rookie driver Greg Coverdale escaped a seven-car pileup to battle on the restart, with Kramer pulling out the victory to make it four wins on the year. Kramer and Greg Coverdale would run much of their URC careers competing against each other and even spent time in Australia racing Sprint Cars as part of Team USA in 1996. Coverdale remembers his early battles with Kramer and running against him:

> My rookie year was 1991 and at that time, Kramer was on top of his game. So pretty much all season I got passed by him. Then, I think we had two weekends left in the season and I won at Bridgeport and I passed Glenn Fitzcharles and Kramer to do it. Over the next three years, I was still driving for my father's team and Kramer was always real quiet at the track. He was definitely serious and had his game face on. Well, me and the crowd I hung around with would heckle him and we got along with him. I always got along with him and never had any problems with him. He was the man to beat. I knew if I did not beat him to the front it was pretty much over.
>
> When we really started getting close to racing each other was in 1993. We had a race at Delaware International Speedway [formerly US 13 Speedway] and Dave McGough checked out on the field. The race went nonstop and I got into second and Kramer started to come on. I always kidded him and called him "Kramminer" because he was always cramming that car into the corner. I could not catch Dave, but all of a sudden, after ten laps, Kramer started showing me his nose like he always does and we raced side-by-side for probably fifteen laps and in the process ran Dave down and passed him. I just happened to get out first and won. I really believe if Kramer had gotten out first he would have walked away from me. He was driving the Fenimore car then.
>
> After that night, we became closer and joked around with each other something awful. I would ask him questions and he was always honest with his answers. He would not tell you anything as far as setup and everything, but he would give you a couple pointers to get you headed in the right direction. That was one of the classic battles in my career. It was just a great race. He was both smooth and aggressive. If he was in the right position, he might squeeze you a little bit, but was not one to hit you. As many times as we raced side-by-side, we only touched wheels maybe two to three times over the years. It was never anything intentional or deliberate; it was just racing. He knew he could trust me and that I was not going to fence him and I knew I could trust him to do the same and [not] stuff me in the wall. Racing with that man was probably the best thing that happened to me in my racing career. It kind of turned me on to do better because I knew what I had to beat and he was one of the all-time greats.

On July 14, 1991, Kramer continued his tear through the month of July, almost sweeping the entire month's races. The URC headed back to Bridgeport Speedway with an impressive field of forty Sprint Cars entered for the night's features. The popular twin-twelve event offered two twelve-lap features run separately at different times during the night's scheduled events. Just as they had done earlier in the season, Kramer and Fitzcharles conquered the night's feature events, winning one race apiece in front of the capacity crowd.

The URC headed up north for their annual Canadian Summer Tour in late July, giving Kramer the chance to add a third country to his win list. Kramer had already won many Sprint Car races in the USA and Australia and was anxious to add Canada to his list as well. On July 26 at the Autodrome Granby, Kramer capitalized on his chance to win in Canada during the URC's first stop of the Canadian tour. Picking off car after car, Kramer wowed the large and enthusiastic Canadian crowd on his way to the win. Going the extra mile for their fans, Kramer and the Fenimore team had flyers printed that included information about the team and Kramer in both English and French so that the French-speaking Canadians could be well informed about Kramer and his racing history.

The Fenimore team celebrates another victory during the URC's Canadian tour. The whole crew, often referred to as the dream team, surround Kramer (with trophy) in Victory Lane.

While Kramer's first race in Canada was one in which he seemed superior to all the other cars on the track, the second race in the Canadian series would be much different, and many would say was the best URC race of the 1991 season. The race, held at the Autodrome Drummond, featured Kramer starting deep in the field and John Jenkins leading the field from the early laps. For the first half of the feature, Kramer picked off cars one by one while racing his way into the second position. Jenkins took to the high groove and Kramer went to his patented low groove to challenge for the lead. The race had several cautions, making for nail-biting restarts as the two raced side-by-side for several laps. On the final lap, a blown engine in another competitor's car caused Jenkins to check up in the final corner, and Kramer just kept the hammer down to blast by the leader and claim the clean sweep of the Canadian races. In a 1991 interview with Cher Zimmerman, Kramer remembered what many said was the best race of the year:

> The hardest win this season was definitely the race with John Jenkins at Drummondville. I tried everything to get past him, so I had to go for broke on the last lap. We raced about ten laps, pulling side-by-side, and even swapping the lead through the turns. I couldn't believe the picture that showed just how close that finish was. I felt bad for Jenkins because he had the race won until the final corner. I guess it was my turn to be the hero that night.

Sharon remembers the success of the Canada trip and trying to get Kramer's mind off racing for a little bit to see Niagara Falls on the way back home from north of the border:

> Kramer liked to relax every now and then. He was good and enjoyed himself once you got him to a place, but it was getting him there that was the challenge. When we went to Canada we had Kurtis and Felecia with us, I said we are going to stop and see Niagara Falls on the way home and he moaned and groaned, but we ended up stopping on the way back. He had a wonderful time and created great memories with the kids going on the boat *Maid of the Mist* and other touristy things. It was just getting him there!

The win in Canada would be Kramer's seventh and final race victory of the year. In the next six races of the URC season, Kramer's consistency helped him clinch his first URC Sprint Car Championship. Kramer's fourth-place finish at Delaware International Speedway, eighth place at Selinsgrove Speedway, third place at Bridgeport Speedway, third at Delaware International Speedway, fourth at Grandview Speedway, and seventh place at Bridgeport Speedway gave him the needed points to secure the coveted championship with one race left to go in the season. That night in a car that was down two cylinders, Kramer was still able to nurse the car home in seventh to clinch his URC point championship. It was the first URC Championship for both Kramer and car owner Henry Fenimore.

The team's stats were impressive for the 1991 season, featuring nineteen top-ten finishes in twenty-four races, including seven race wins. On his way to winning the URC Championship, Kramer also won the Triple Crown events, smaller URC championship events that rewarded the top points finishing driver at races in Delaware, New Jersey and Pennsylvania. Those titles included the DL Motors Pennsylvania Point Series, the Bash Engines Delaware State Series and the Fairgrounds Square Mall Triple Crown Championship in the URC. Not only had Kramer won the championship, but the only thing that was damaged on the car the whole year was one side rail that got bent at McKean County. Doug Wolfgang remembered Kramer's URC years and why his ability to stay out of trouble was so important to his success:

> The URC was no walk in the rose garden back then. Guys like Buckley, Glenn Fitzcharles and Dave Kelly made that series really tough. One thing that happens to a lot of guys is that along the line something goes wrong and you break an arm or break a leg and you get scared. Then your desire to ache on Monday morning goes away, and Kramer never really got injured, so that's a testament to his ability. He raced longer than most because he never hurt himself so bad when he was younger. He didn't hurt himself because he was good at what he did and knew what he could do and what he could not do in a race car. That's a huge amount of ability to be able to recognize and do that.

The smooth yet aggressive driver made it through the whole season without one wreck, leaving much of the team's spares and equipment in good order for the next race season.

Kramer's brother George remembers Kramer's attitude during his running with the URC:

> I don't think Kramer had any more fun than when he was running for the URC because that was a very, very fun, everyone-works-together crowd. He really liked that. Kramer had gone through a lot of rides and there are only so many. He lost a couple of rides, but most of them he quit and that was okay because there was another ride waiting for him to do better at. Once he went through all those and there were no more left, that's when the URC ride became available for Kramer. Then you really saw his true appreciation

for people appreciating him. I think people appreciate him now as well, but at the time it was just hard to describe how he was so young, so immediate to succeed and made it look so easy. It upset a lot of people due to his instant success. They thought, how could he sit here and do so well when we have been racing for so much longer? He blew their doors off, and that was that natural talent shining through.

Kramer gives the camera a smile as he awaits another feature event. Kramer easily became one of racing's most loved personalities with his smooth style and easygoing attitude both on and off the track.

Kramer found himself at home on the traveling circus that was the URC Sprint Car series. The feeling of being appreciated by his peers and the family atmosphere attracted the now forty-two-year-old father of two to stay in the series. With two children growing up and now in school, the weekends traveling to the races provided family time during the drives, and that was something Kramer really enjoyed. As always, when you saw Kramer at the track, not far behind were wife Sharon, son Kurtis and daughter Felecia. Former URC president John Zimmerman remembers what it was like in the URC in those days:

> At the time, it was a real family atmosphere. We always had a good time and Kramer was pretty serious at the track, but at the banquets, let's just say he got his money's worth. He enjoyed his fellow competitors. There was one time when Jimmy Martin got mad at Kramer because he thought Kramer hit him on the track. After reviewing the video, Martin realized it was not Kramer who did, it so Martin sent Kramer a rose with a card that

139

said "Roses are red, violets are blue, I saw the film and it wasn't you." Kramer got a big kick out of that. So Kramer being Kramer, he gets rid of the card before Sharon gets home and made his own card up and gave the rose to Sharon. Sharon's response was, "What did you do?"

Even though Fenimore and Kramer had a successful first season together in 1991, neither would comment on a return to defend the title late that year. Fenimore commented on the thought process of making a return to defend the URC title and running a full-time Sprint Car operation in a 1991 interview with Bev Thompson. When asked if Kramer would return, Fenimore replied, "It's Kramer's ride if he wants it." When asked if they would run full-time, he commented on the reasons that would make the tough decision: "A lot depends on the rule changes and the economy, but we will be back with URC, I'm just not sure how much or how little." Later that year, both Fenimore and Kramer agreed to return as a team and defend their URC title by running a full schedule for 1992.

One of the reasons for Fenimore's and Kramer's quick and consistent success in the URC was the top-notch team that Fenimore had put together. Knowing the quality of the Fenimore team was a deciding factor in Kramer's decision to pursue a second championship. The #28 B&F Towing Team members included Biddy Winward, who took care of the motors; Bob Powell, who looked after the chassis; John Carmen, Gino Jamison and Butch Moore. Together, they were the glue that helped hold together such a talented bunch of individuals. In his own words, Kramer tells how important they were in his success from 1991 to 1993:

> I must give credit to my crew. The B&F Towing #28 team does all the work and gets very little recognition. Henry Fenimore and his crew are absolutely the best in the business. It's just like football. All you ever hear about is the quarterback, but it is really a team effort. I'm just the quarterback and it's high time to give the rest of the team credit. These guys spend so much time working on the car and motor, it's almost indescribable. I can only get to Henry's once a week or so because it's a two-hour ride one way for me. Everything depends on the rest of the team.

With the 1991 championship behind them, the team set their sights on the 1992 URC Championship. The season consisted of only sixteen race events in 1992. The short season meant that consistency would be key and put an even greater emphasis on winning. Kramer and the Fenimore crew got off to a rough start in the first two events. A flat tire ended his winning chances at the season opener at Delaware International Speedway. Although the team jumped in and repaired the tire, Kramer came out a lap down and was not able to make up the distance to finish high in the standings that night. The very next week, Kramer won his heat race at Bridgeport Speedway, but hurt the engine, resulting in a speedy engine swap before the main feature of the night's events. With all hands on deck, the Fenimore crew finished the swap just in time for the feature. Kramer moved steadily up the ladder in this race, all the way to the fourth position, just shy of the top three.

The next stop on the 1992 URC tour was Fonda Speedway in Fonda, New York. For the second week in a row, the #28 Sprinter blew an engine in practice, and Kramer had to rely on his crew to get him back up to speed. The team had a new engine back in the car for Kramer to race in the third qualifying heat and win. Kramer started ninth and was up to fourth by lap number five. It only took a few more laps for Kramer to pass the race leader, Paul Moltz, and stretch his lead till the checkered flag waved. It was an important win for Kramer because he had never won at Fonda before in his long career. It was a great victory for the entire team, and it was truly the entire team that won that night at Fonda.

The team was back on track and followed up the win with another great showing at Weedsport Speedway in Weedsport, New York. Kramer started in the twentieth position and was charging as hard as he could, but ran out of time to finish just short of first place. The back-to-back one-two finish gave the team the consistency they were looking for and put them back in the points contention with twelve races to go in the season. Kramer once again was the runner-up at Bridgeport Speedway on June 7, 1992, and was back in Victory Lane when the URC once again made a stop at Delaware International Speedway in late June. The twenty-five-lap feature event saw thirty-four Sprint Cars in all registered for competition. Kramer won his heat and led much of the feature, holding off a hard-charging Greg Coverdale to win his second feature event of the year.

The next week Kramer went back-to-back for the first time in 1992, winning at Orange County Speedway in Middletown, New York. Crew chief Biddy Winward gambled on using a much harder tire and knew that the car would come into its own near the end of the race. Sure enough, on lap eighteen, after appearing to gain no ground on leader

Jimmy Martin, Kramer's car came alive and noticeably started reeling in Martin. On lap twenty-two, Kramer raced past Martin and won his third race of the year. A flat tire at Bridgeport Speedway put a damper on Kramer's championship hopes for the year as he lost valuable points in the mid-season stretch before the URC tour headed to Canada for their annual tour. At the first Canadian race in Autodrome Granby in Quebec, Kramer finished a solid third in the twenty-five lap feature.

In the second race of the series, Kramer found himself back in familiar territory. Lapping all but nine cars, Kramer raced his way to victory, and more importantly, back into contention for the URC Championship. The record crowd witnessed the twenty-five-lap event go nonstop as Kramer expertly navigated lapped traffic on his way to his fourth win of the year. With four races left in the season, the championship was shaping up to be a three-way battle between Kramer, Jim Baker and Dave McGough. The pressure was on in the last four races, and winning or finishing up front would be critical for anyone wishing to bring home the 1992 URC Championship.

The next race was held at Delaware International Speedway and was dominated by Greg Coverdale, who had had a tough go of it in Canada, breaking a rear end one night and suffering a hard crash the next. Kramer averted disaster during the race when, during a red flag, son Kurt spotted a flat tire on his dad's car while he was sitting on the track waiting to re-fire. Kramer, who was in sixth at the time, had to pit to change tires, putting him last on the next restart. Battling back, Kramer finished in fourth place and saved a disastrous points night with help from the keen eye of Kurt. At the next race at Bridgeport Speedway, Kramer made it look easy as he was unchallenged, taking his fifth win of the year and twenty-sixth career win in the URC.

The win gave Kramer a comfortable points lead going into the final two races of the season, but the team took no chances and meticulously prepared the car each week to avoid any surprises. Henry Fenimore explains the importance of the team maintenance program:

> The very next day after the race, the car must be stripped and the motor serviced. I know it is sometimes a burden, especially after a long tow weekend, but problems must be dealt with early in the week. We've also practiced motor changes, so we are prepared for this emergency at the track. No one gets in the way, although it may look like a mass of men hovering over the car. We know each other's moves to such a point that we can work that closely together.

Always prepared, the team used a backup car in the next-to-last race of the year at Bridgeport to finish eighth and stay ahead in the points, leading into the final race of the year at Georgetown Speedway in Georgetown, Delaware.

At the final race of the year, Kramer was on his way to victory and the points championship when the motor expired, ending the team's hopes for winning the final race of the season and putting their points championship in jeopardy. Fortunately, no other team in contention for the championship was able to finish high enough in the final race to unseat the #28 Fenimore team at the top, and Kramer could now be called a two-time URC Champion. In what was a roller-coaster season, Kramer won five out of the sixteen races on his way to his second consecutive URC title.

After the championship, car owner Fenimore commented on his driver, Kramer.

> He is an incredible race car driver. It is just so easy to work with a person like him. Kramer is not demanding and is easy on equipment. His knowledge is so valuable. Kramer can relate to the team so well, and let them know exactly what the car is doing. He makes no demand for change, but instead relies on their expertise based on his input.

Whatever the magic owner/driver combination was, Kramer and Fenimore found it during the 1991 and 1992 race seasons. Kramer was finding his time in the URC to be some of the most enjoyable he had ever experienced in his racing career.

Son Kurtis was now getting his hands dirty helping crew his dad's ride, and daughter Felecia was very visible in the pits, always her dad's biggest fan and cheering him on every race. Felecia remembers her routine of helping her dad get ready for a race:

> It was a whole routine to get Dad ready. I always had to yell at him when it was time for him to go out on the track because he didn't pay attention—he was too busy thinking about what to do with the car to go faster. I would take the helmet and gloves; next, he would get in the car and I would make sure the belts were nice and flat. Then he would perfectly position the steering wheel and I would always pull on it at least twice to make sure it was locked in and tight. Then he would put his helmet and gloves on. He also had a helmet strap that hooked to his uniform and I would put that on.
>
> Later, when we got older, the radio was the big deal. We would fight about that all the time. He had the custom ear buds, but I still had to tape them in onto his ear (with pink duct tape, of course) and he would give me a hard time that they weren't comfortable or whatever.

When Dad and I went to the track to watch a race, he called it father/daughter bonding time. He was bubbly, outgoing and would talk to anyone. If we were racing ourselves, he would stay in the trailer and would not venture out to talk to many people. He would keep to himself a lot and you could see the wheels spinning in his head constantly. He sat on the wheel well like a bench and you could see how focused he was. He would only leave the trailer to go look at the track to make his plan for the car based on the track conditions.

Kramer's second URC Championship was super-popular with the fans as well. Kramer's popularity with the fans was at an all-time high during his time with the URC. Perhaps it was because of his already legendary career; perhaps people liked rooting for the perceived older guy racing (even though Kramer was only forty-three at the end of the 1992 season); and perhaps fans just liked who Kramer was. His daughter Felecia offers her opinions as to why her dad became so endeared to his fans and fellow competitors:

While taking racing very seriously on the track, Kramer loved to relax and have a good time when away from his racing duties. At the 1992 URC Award Ceremony, Kramer dressed the part to celebrate his second URC Championship.

From a fan perspective he was always available and willing to sign autographs. He really liked hanging out and talking to fans. He had the ability to make everyone feel very special and he understood that if you didn't have fans in the grandstands, that there wouldn't be a race. Dad did a really good job with that. As far as the racers, they would always ask Dad questions because he had been around for so long and had so much knowledge for others to learn from. He loved helping others learn more about racing. Dad was just so smart about these race cars. Mom and I used to joke around and say if Dad was not racing he would be miserable so we were happy to see him race for so long. He would always think about who he was passing, what was that driver's signature move, what he should be careful of around other drivers, and he would study and watch stuff like that. He was a very brave guy. The best thing about Dad is that he was so humble about all his accomplishments. He never made Kurt or I think we were special just because our dad was Kramer. We were just like any other race fan at the track cheering on that pink race car.

The popular driver was now the two-time back-to-back defending URC Sprint Car Champion, and he headed into 1993 looking for a remarkable three-peat. Not wanting to end a good thing, Kramer and Henry Fenimore decided to continue their successful relationship as driver and car owner for yet another year.

The 1993 season would be a year of change and turbulence in the URC series. Most of the controversy was over URC's spec tires and the addition of asphalt tracks to the 1993 URC schedule. A man named Butch Kaelin was the Hoosier Tire distributor in the URC area and had taken a keen interest in making sure that the URC included some new paved speedways on their 1993 schedule. While many saw the promise of expanding the URC's exposure to new venues, others saw it as simply a ploy for Kaelin to sell more tires. The controversy split the URC and put the series in turmoil as Butch Kaelin became the new URC president for the year. Many were concerned that rich owners would dominate the asphalt races with cars specifically designed for paved speedways, while the teams who were on a budget could simply not afford the specialized equipment. After all was said and done, Kaelin used his new position to include two pavement races. Apple Valley Speedway and Flemington were added to the 1993 schedule and would have a direct impact on who would be the 1993 URC Champion.

Kramer started off the season finishing third at Delaware International Speedway behind second-place Fran Hogue and first-place finisher and Delaware native Greg Coverdale. Charlie Cathell, the owner and promoter of Delaware International Speedway, watched Kramer's URC career from his first visit to Delaware in the Fiore #8 till the end of his career running his own #73 in 2013. Cathell remembers how valuable Kramer's experience was on the track:

> He turned left a whole bunch of times in his career. I look at it this way. I know in motor sports as you get older your timing gets off, but I have sat here and watched guys who people consider up there in age. I'll use Kramer and Hal Browning as examples. Sure, their timing may be off a bit, but they certainly make up for it in experience. I watched Kramer run and just sat back and waited for the young guy to make a mistake and then drive on by while the other drivers watched and tried to figure out how they got passed. That's stuff you can't go by out of a book. It's your butt in the seat and your hands on the steering wheel with years and years of experience.

The URC made a rare appearance in North Carolina for the next race at 311 Speedway. Kramer again would nail down a solid second-place finish, starting his season off consistently and racking up valuable points for the championship. After another win by the emerging Greg Coverdale at Fonda Speedway, the URC headed to the Cayuga County Fairgrounds, where Kramer would pick up his first victory of the 1993 season. Kramer and runner-up Jim Baker touched wheels several times during the twenty-five-lap feature, but both continued, with Kramer collecting the hard-fought win.

Kramer collected his second win of the season two weeks later at SeaCoast Speedway (same track as Georgetown Speedway) in Georgetown, Delaware, on June 25, 1993. Kramer's only competition was Midge Miller, whom Kramer overpowered mid-race on his way to a dominating win at the half-mile speedway. Kramer would post another runner-up position at Delaware International Speedway in the very next race, keeping him at the head of the URC points race in 1993. Georgetown Speedway and Delaware International Speedway were just miles from one another, so the Williamson family sometimes stayed the night in the area after Friday's race at Georgetown and would go to Delaware International the next day. Sharon Williamson remembers being the commander in chief and a jam Kramer got himself into during one visit to the First State:

> We were staying overnight in Delaware. We ran Georgetown and we were running Delaware International the next day. Checkout at the motel was 11:00 a.m. I was yelling at everyone to get moving. Kramer called me sergeant because I was always yelling at everyone to get moving. Kramer

always slept in as long as I would let him. I finally told him, "Kramer, let's go." I said, "Checkout is at 11:00 a.m., go get your shower." He said real smart to me, "What the hell are they going to do? Shut the water off?" So Kramer got in the shower while the kids and I were taking our bags out to the truck. All of a sudden I hear Kramer yelling, "Sharon!" I went into the bathroom and he was on his knees in the shower trying to splash water on his head to rinse the soap out of his hair. The water shut off! It turned out there was a water main break in the area and they had to shut the water off at the motel. It was so funny because of what he said earlier. I still laugh to this day when I tell this story. Let's just say, he listened better after this happened.

Staying over between races spared the long ride home back to Pennsylvania and saved valuable travel money that the team could then put back into the car. Sharon remembers those long rides home from the races that seemed even longer when things did not go just quite right:

When things didn't go right at the races, it was sometimes a long ride home. I was always giving the kids looks in the back seat to just sit there

Kramer with daughter Felecia and son Kurtis, relaxing during a break in the racing action. Family was always first with the Williamsons.

and keep quiet. I would usually pack an emergency food bag. The kids and I liked to stop on the way home and eat. If Kramer had a bad night, he wouldn't stop, or if he knew I had food with us, he would just say we could eat that. So, I would pack an emergency food bag; that way, if he didn't stop, the kids could crawl in the back of the truck and have something to eat. I guess we were punishing him for punishing the kids and me. Of course, when we got home, I would have to make him a sandwich, but the kids would get so mad at him.

Such was life on the road with the traveling URC Series and the kind of life Kramer had lived since he was a youngster: always on the move, roaming from town to town racing Sprint Cars anytime and anywhere.

That is, until July 11, 1993, when the #28 team took a stand against the inclusion of two asphalt tracks in the year's schedule. Owner Henry Fenimore and Kramer sat out the July race at Apple Valley, New York, in protest. By any measure, the experiment on asphalt was a flop. Only thirteen cars showed up to race that night, and as predicted, the race was won by an outsider, Gary Hieber, driving a specialty Sprint Car designed for pavement only. The lack of cars definitely made a statement, but by skipping the race, the #28 Fenimore Team put themselves in a big hole for the URC Championship that year, earning zero points for not racing. The URC returned to the surface they were meant for, dirt, on July 17, 1993, at Bridgeport, New Jersey. Kramer started a trend of three straight victories that night that would last the whole month of July, giving him a clean sweep of every race he entered. His first of those victories came on the heels of tragedy as the racing world learned about the passing of NASCAR star Davey Allison. Allison, who was a huge fan favorite, was killed in a helicopter crash at Talladega Speedway. Kramer and Davey Allison shared the same #28 race car number, so it was fitting in Victory Lane when Kramer dedicated his win to Davey and all the race fans who loved him.

As the dog days of summer approached, it was time for the URC to escape the summer heat and head back north of the border for their annual Canadian tour. The tour visited its regular tracks, the Autodrome Granby and the Autodrome Drummond. At Granby, Kramer won by a thread, literally. Kramer inherited the lead from Jon Eldreth, who had a rear end go out, and Fran Hogue, who blew a right rear. While leading, Kramer's Sprint Car began to miss badly and caused great concern amongst the crew. Kramer nursed the car to victory, finding out later that the coil wire was just hanging on by a thread. The win was Kramer's fourth win of the season and helped pull him back into the points battle with Dave McGough.

At the next race in the Canadian tour, at Drummondville, Kramer dominated the race, passing leader Tom Capie as he pulled clear and went on to his fifth win of the season, sweeping every race run on dirt in July. The URC headed back to the States for competition at Delaware International Speedway to start out the month of August. While it was one of Kramer's favorite tracks, he was forced to retire early after mechanical ills took him out of the competition that night. Kramer finished a dismal twenty-third, but he did get to watch URC history made that evening. Mares Stellfox became the first female winner in URC history on August 7, 1993. The popular victory paved the way for more female drivers and winners in the URC, like Judi Bates and Becca Anderson.

The URC headed back to the blacktop for one last time in 1993 at Flemington Speedway in New Jersey. Again, Kramer and the Fenimore team would not run at all in the evening's event. The race was won again by Gary Hieber driving an asphalt Sprint Car in a field of only seventeen race cars. All the ground that Kramer made up in July by winning three races in a row was quickly erased as the team again had a zero-point night. This would be the last race on asphalt for the URC; while the club had run on paved surfaces from 1948 through 1974, the series would never again visit a blacktop track in its history.

The next race was back on the dirt surface of Bridgeport Speedway. Points leader Dave McGough, who ran both asphalt races, exited the race early with mechanical problems, opening the door for Kramer to gain back some valuable points. Greg Coverdale wowed fans with his aggressive rim-riding style and took the lead late in the race with a hard-charging Kramer right behind him. Kramer gave it all he had, but Coverdale came out on top, with Kramer grabbing big points for his second-place finish. Kramer's runner-up finish, coupled with Coverdale's win and McGough's early breakdown, put the top four in points only 180 points from each other. For the rest of the season, it would be a four-way battle for the URC Championship.

As the points battle tightened up and the season was nearing its end, Kramer won his sixth race of the year in what some called his toughest win in the URC, ever. Kramer started in the back of the field and was fighting an ill-handling race car for most of the night. Amazingly,

Kramer worked himself up through the field and up to second place behind race leader Jim Baker by lap twenty of twenty-five. Kramer made quick work of Baker and would go on to win one of the most hard-fought feature wins of his career. The championship would come down to the last three races of the year, and despite skipping the two races held on asphalt, Kramer was right in the thick of the championship contenders.

On September 18, 1993, the URC headed to Delaware International Speedway for their last appearance of the year. With the points battle so close, all the competitors brought out their A game heading into the race. The night's action did not disappoint fans as Mike Haggenbottom was leading the race while Kramer was locked in a fierce battle with Dave McGough. Going into a corner on the last lap, Kramer and McGough got too close and touched wheels, sending both cars into a spin until they stopped on the speedway. The night would end up a practical wash in points for both drivers, neither one gaining on the other heading into the final two races of the year. At the second-to-last race, at Fonda Speedway in New York, Kramer and Dave McGough would again battle it out for the race win and championship. The duo finished one and two, with McGough claiming the top position and Kramer coming home in second place for the evening's feature event. While McGough held a slight edge heading into the final race at Bridgeport Speedway, it was still possible for Kramer to catch the points leader in the final event of the year.

During the last feature event of the year, Kramer gave his all in an effort to claim the title and race win. Greg Coverdale jumped out to the race lead early on, while Kramer and McGough battled their way through the field. The door was left open just a bit for Kramer to regain the title when McGough dropped out early with mechanical problems. Kramer raced his way to second place and challenged Coverdale for the rest of the race, but could not complete the pass before the checkered flag fell. In one of the closest points battles in URC history, Dave McGough won the 1993 URC Championship over Kramer by a mere sixteen points.

Sometimes taking a stand for what you believe in has a price, and the price for the #28 Fenimore team's skipping the two asphalt races was losing the 1993 URC Championship. If the team had even just shown up and cruised around in last place, they would have claimed their third championship in a row. However, cruising around for points is not in the blood of a true racer, and both Kramer and Fenimore were racers who raced to win. The team took a stand based on what they thought was right and one certainly has to respect that decision, even though the cost of that decision was quite high. Even finishing second, the team could hold their head up high with six wins on the season, more than anyone else in the series that year, and a second place in the URC Championship for 1993. The second place was a testament to Kramer's attitude of never giving up and always striving for the win, even in times of seemingly insurmountable obstacles.

The combination of Kramer's driving and Henry Fenimore's first-class Sprint Car seemed like a partnership that would go on and on for years to come. However, all good things come to an end, and after the awards ceremony for the 1993 Championship, the two decided to go their separate ways. After enjoying three years of success and stability in the URC with the Fenimore team, Kramer was now a free agent and was looking for another top-notch Sprint Car ride. If fans of Sprint Car racing thought Kramer's first three years in the URC were impressive, the next two would define the grit and determination of Kramer as he would pilot a car that most said would never have a chance of winning a race in the URC, let alone winning a championship.

After Kramer and Fenimore parted company, Kramer put his name out there to see who was looking for a quality Sprint Car pilot and who had a team that could contend for a third URC Championship. Enter car owner Vince Gangemi. Gangemi fell in love with stock cars as a teenager and worked on several pit crews, learning the ins and outs of racing hands-on. A Ford fanatic since the age of fifteen, Gangemi was also a huge fan of Scats Anfuso, who fielded Ford-powered Sprint Cars in the URC for many years. As an owner, Anfuso won over one hundred races in Ford-powered cars, often against the dominant Chevrolets of the time. Gangemi would eventually want to win races and championships with his own Ford-powered Sprint Cars.

He first witnessed the awesome power of Sprint Cars when the URC visited Bridgeport Speedway and he was hooked instantly. Gangemi remembers his first experience watching the URC and buying his first Sprint Car:

> I fell in love with the Sprint Cars. They were so much faster and wilder than stock cars. I bought my first Sprint Car from Bill Brian, which was a Gambler.

One reason for the Gambler was because it was a wide bar car and it would be able to house a Ford motor. I didn't start with a Ford. I actually started with a Chevy because I couldn't find or afford what I wanted at that time. In 1990, I bought the heads and parts, then Scats helped us put together our first Ford.

Gangemi's first foray into introducing Ford back into Sprint Car racing was a tough one. In 1992, the team flipped back and forth between Ford and Chevy power during the year. They also flipped drivers as well. Gary Gollub and Gangemi's brother Sam shared seats during the year, and the only award they won was the "URC Hard Luck Award," not exactly the award you want to receive at the end of the year. The next year in 1993, while Kramer was racing for Henry Fenimore, the Gangemi team found a steady driver in Stew Brown, but were still flipping between Ford and Chevrolet power. At the end of the 1993 season, Gangemi decided it was time to go all-in running the Ford and make a serious commitment to winning races and a possible URC Championship.

In 1994, Kramer became Gangemi's first hired gun, and the two would set their sights on winning races and bringing Ford back to Victory Lane in the Chevrolet-dominated URC series. It was a huge leap of faith for Kramer, who was used to having the top ride in the URC for the last three years driving the #28 Fenimore car. Now, jumping into the #84 Gangemi Sprint Car, which had little proven success, seemed like a huge chance to take for the former URC Champion. Nevertheless, the duo set forth into uncharted territory at the beginning of the 1994 URC season with much optimism.

That optimism soon changed to despair as the team's start to the season was a disaster. A steady stream of DNFs kept the team from finishing many of the events, and when the team did finish, the Ford motor trouble was still evident. At Fonda Speedway, the team showed signs of promise by finishing fourth, but it was obvious to those watching the motor was going sour, forcing the Gangemi team to change motors in the parking lot of the Howard Johnson after the race. While the team was trying their best, the pressure was starting to mount and rumors were starting to spread that if the team continued to perform poorly, Kramer was going to leave. Kramer, who was known for switching rides frequently, decided to stay and help the team work out their engine issues. In a 1995 interview, Kramer remembers the frustration during that time:

Every time I'd be sitting in the infield while everyone else was out there racing, I'd say no more, no more. But I made a deal for the season and I knew if we could just get a few bugs worked out, we'd be okay. I can be a very difficult person. Vince gave me the best of everything, new tires each race or whatever it took to win. Al Rozzelle continued to squeeze more and more horsepower from the Ford. But I am the type of person who gets frustrated very easily when mistakes happen that could have been avoided.

Even though everyone was dedicated to the goal of winning a race, with frustrations mounting, car owner Gangemi describes the pressure he felt during the time.

You hire a driver like Kramer Williamson, someone who has had the best of rides, and you can't provide a car that finishes a race. I knew Kramer was frustrated, and that made us work even harder to achieve our goal. He is a very demanding driver, but I told myself that it comes with the territory, when you have that caliber of driver on your team. If he wasn't so demanding, he probably wouldn't be the driver he is today. It is hard sometimes when you have so many people on the team, and everyone has an idea. You can't always accommodate everyone's ideas.

During those first races of the 1994 season, Gangemi was told by many respectable owners to put a Chevrolet engine in his car, but Gangemi's response to those people was, "No, I can't. I can't give up all the time and effort." Perhaps Kramer saw something he liked in Gangemi's grit and determination to win.

In the fifth race of the 1994 URC season, things would finally click for the team, and Kramer would give Gangemi a gift for which he had been waiting. On May 30, 1994, the URC rolled into Dundee, New York, during the northern swing of their tour. The Ford motor seemed to be working flawlessly as the crew prepared for the night's qualifying events. The race, titled the ESS/URC Challenge, featured drivers from both Sprint Car series combined into one exciting event. Kramer, benefiting from a good starting position in the front row, battled USS Craig Keel in the twenty-five-lap feature. Keel would even get past Kramer at one point for the lead on the backstretch, only to have Kramer grab it back in the corner. Kramer finally pulled ahead towards the end of the race and won his first race of the 1994 season. The win was owner Vince Gangemi's first win in URC and the first time in fourteen years a Ford-powered car won in URC competition. The victory was a huge relief for Gangemi, who had fielded a car in the URC for six years. In a 1994 interview with Cher Zimmerman, Gangemi relived the feelings of winning that first race:

I was completely shocked. I kept thinking we had a good shot with a front row starting spot, but I've had my hopes crushed so many times that I wasn't at all that positive that we were going to win. I watched Kramer take the lead and I knew Keel was going to be tough. Then the race came to a stop. I knew it was toward the end of the race, but I thought maybe it was just a caution. The track was so dusty that I was unable to see the flagman. Then I saw the cars coming off the track, and only at that point did I realize we won the race.

The joy of victory would be short-lived as the team continued to struggle with engine problems again after their first victory of the year. Refusing to give up, the team worked hard at making the Ford power plant more reliable. Their efforts were rewarded on June 2, 1994, at Delaware International Speedway. Unlike the first win of the season when Kramer won the feature from a first-row starting spot, Kramer would have to come through the field from twenty-first starting position to have a chance for his second victory of the year. The team was finally starting to figure out the powerful Ford motor, and Kramer made quick work of racing his way through the field to the front of the pack. Moving into second, Kramer patiently waited for leader Tom Capie to catch lapped traffic. A lapped car that broke the leader's rhythm was all that was needed for the experienced veteran to seize the opportunity and take the lead for good. Kramer had put the #84 Gangemi Sprint Car back into Victory Lane for the second time in 1994.

With two victories in the record books for 1994, the #84 Gangemi team continued to struggle for the consistency needed to be a championship contender. The team fell on hard times again during the annual URC visit to Canada; however, this time the engine ran fine, and two crashes would be to blame for the poor finishes. Although known for not wrecking or being hard on equipment, Kramer was uncharacteristically involved in two hard accidents during the Canadian tour. After a small crash at Autodrome Granby, the team had a very serious crash at Autodrome Drummondville. After Kramer won his heat, all seemed well for the final. During the night's feature event, Kramer flipped the #84 several times in spectacular fashion. Although Kramer escaped injury, the car was a total loss. The Shaw chassis was completely destroyed, and the Ford power plant was damaged as well— sticking a major blow to a team that was already spending more money than many of the other teams because of their allegiance to Ford. Many speculated that it cost three times more to run a Ford than a Chevrolet.

Owner Vince Gangemi explains in a 1994 interview with Cher Zimmerman:

> That's partially right. What cost was the research and trial and error. Knowing what we need to know, I can build a Ford for the same cost as a Chevy. It's tough when no one else knows what to do. It took four years, but it was definitely worth it [winning a race]. I spent an unbelievable amount of time on the phone calling all over the country to gather information from Ford owners.

With the car totaled, the team went back to the drawing board and used the experience gained in the first part of the year to construct a more Ford-friendly Sprint Car. While the motor was damaged, it was not a total loss. Ace mechanic and motor builder Al Rozzelle went to work repairing what was left of the Ford power plant. The Shaw chassis, on the other hand, was destroyed, and the team needed a backup. Kramer had started to build a new chassis at the beginning of the year, but it was unfinished at the time of the accident. Kramer went to work putting the finishing touches on the frame in just a few short days. The frame was a unique creation, as Kramer describes in a 1994 interview. "We used the same chassis in '94 and '95. None of the big chassis people would build a low rail for a Ford. We wanted more motor set-back than normal. So I built what we needed. I actually built two, but one never saw the track." The idea was to have a spare chassis in case the primary car was wrecked. The team simply never needed the spare chassis for the rest of '94 and '95, mostly due to Kramer's ability to avoid trouble with his patience and experience.

The team and Kramer impressively had the car back on track for the next week's race at Delaware International Speedway. The team was fast right out of the box, posting a second-place finish in their first night of shaking down a completely new Sprint Car. Running at West Virginia Speedway, located in Parkersburg, for the first time in URC history, Kramer put on quite a show during the night's feature event. Starting deep in the field due to a flat tire during qualifying, Kramer navigated through the field en route to winning the night's twenty-five-lap main event. The team had now won three races and were slowly becoming more consistent with their motor program and the addition of a new chassis.

As the end of the season drew near, the team concentrated on winning as many races as they could. Well out of the points championship contest due to their early season inconsistencies, the #84 team wanted to end their season on a high note to send them into the 1995 season with enough confidence to contend for a championship. On October 15, 1994, URC visited Bridgeport Speedway for the second-to-last race of the season. It had taken all season, but the team had the car perfect for the night's race, and Kramer rocketed from the back of the field to the front and simply left the other competitors behind in dominating fashion. People were now starting to talk about the new Ford and its power. When running, the #84 team finished no worse than seventh place in any race during the year. It was the DNFs that killed their points championship hopes. Now with the car staying together consistently, the rest of the URC competitors took notice of the #84 team.

The last race of the year, the Gangemi #84 Sprint Car was again the dominant car of the night. Kramer blew by the field, coming from twelfth starting position to first in just four laps. It would be his fifth victory of the year driving for Gangemi and his thirty-seventh win in URC competition. In just one season, Kramer transformed a winless team running the only Ford in the URC into a five-time feature winner. Gangemi commented on Kramer's impact on the team during an interview shortly after the 1994 season with Cher Zimmerman:

> He changed the complexion of our team. He is a demanding driver, but that caliber of driver is allowed to be. Kramer has a real feel for the car and can adapt to any situation. It is surprising how little we changed the car. Kramer is always thinking of ways to make the car run better. He's serious when he needs to be, but can also be a real cut-up with the guys. We were sitting at the garage on a Wednesday night, our scheduled maintenance night on the car, and Kramer stopped by at the usual time. Since the car was done, the guys planned on a night of bench racing with some of Ink's Pizza. Next thing we know, Kramer starts staring at the car. He thought of a better idea for the wing brackets, then another idea popped into his head. Well, needless to say, we put in a full night of work on the race car.

Kramer was not the only Williamson making a contribution to the Gangemi Team. His son Kurt was also a vital part of the team, helping with setups and learning from his father on a daily basis. Kurtis was now thirteen and absorbing everything he could about racing from his father. "It is amazing at Kurt's age what his father has taught him," commented owner Vince Gangemi.

Ending the year winning the last two races certainly lit a fire under everyone to put an emphasis on competing for the URC Championship

The Gangemi team joins Kramer in Victory Lane. From left to right are: Dave Daniels, Vince Gangemi, Kramer Williamson, Kurt Williamson, John Gangemi and Al Rossetti.

in 1995. Despite their inconsistent finishes in 1994, the team still was able to finish an impressive fifth place in URC points at the end of the year, winning five races along the way. With the season-ending success, Kramer and the #84 Gangemi team decided they had come too far to stop now and stayed together for a run at the championship.

The 1995 season would be a very interesting year in the URC. Glenn Fitzcharles returned to the URC as a full-time driver behind the wheel of Kramer's old ride, the Henry Fenimore #28 Sprint Car. Kramer was ecstatic about the news, as he had wanted to battle the URC legend head-to-head during his previous championships, but the two were never able establish a yearlong battle for URC supremacy. The URC also decided in 1995 to host its first wingless show since 1970. The management at Grandview Speedway approached the URC with the idea of the one-time wingless event for the 1995 season and the URC membership gave it the thumbs up.

For the first three events of the 1995 season, Kramer found the consistency he lacked in the previous year's season. In the season-opening race at Cumberland Raceway, Kramer had a dramatic battle with 1994 URC Champion Greg Coverdale. The two battled until the last lap, with Coverdale inching out the win in dramatic fashion. Races two and three of the year were held at Delaware International Speedway and featured Kramer coming from deep in the pack to finish in the runner-up position. A third-place finish would come at Fonda Speedway before Kramer finally found Victory Lane again at Natural Bridge Speedway in Virginia. Kramer took the lead late in the race from then leader Jerry Dinnen to score his first win of the year and extend his lead in the season's points championship. In the next few events, title contenders Greg Coverdale and Glenn Fitzcharles would both score victories, but the consistent run of Kramer Williamson continued with finishes no worse than sixth place, and more importantly, none of the DNFs that had plagued the team in 1994.

Kramer's next win came on July 8, 1995, on his home turf of Selinsgrove Speedway near his home in Pennsylvania. Some forty-two Sprint Cars showed up for the United Racing Club/Empire Super Sprints Challenge Series race. The race featured cars from both series. Kramer made URC fans proud by winning the twenty-five-lap feature event in fine form, recording his second win of the year in the Gangemi #84. The very next week, and with a home-field advantage on the tracks he had run so much earlier in his career, Kramer won at the historic Williams Grove Speedway. The win brought his run of top-five finishes to eleven races in a row, an incredible change from the season before when the team had so many DNFs. The Gangemi crew had the Ford power plant figured out and running on all cylinders. The win at Williams Grove Speedway was also Kramer's fortieth victory in the URC, an incredible number that he would add to over his next fifteen years of racing.

While the win at Williams Grove Speedway and eleven top-five finishes helped to stretch his points lead, the streak would come to an end in Canada as the URC made their annual tour up north. After he was involved in a three-car accident at Autodrome Granby, Kramer's winning streak came to an end and the points battle tightened. On the second race of the Canadian tour at Autodrome Drummond, Kramer finished a solid third, putting him right back in the picture for the points championship.

Kramer awaits the next race in the driver's seat of the #84 Gangemi car. The team won five features their first year together in 1994 and scored four wins in 1995.

After a one-week break, the URC was back in the States at a never-before-visited speedway. The Pennsylvania Motor Speedway in Pittsburgh suited the powerful Ford motor and Kramer's driving style. The combo blasted from twelfth to second in just five laps. After a multi-lap side-by-side battle with Jon Eldreth, Kramer pulled ahead to capture his fourth and final win of the 1995 season. Kramer had extended family living close by who attended and got to see him pick up the win. On September 2, Kramer finished runner-up to Greg Coverdale at Delaware International Speedway in an epic race that also included Glenn Fitzcharles. The second-place finish allowed Kramer to claim the 1995 Taylor & Messick Delaware State Point Series crown as well as extend his lead in the URC Championship standings. The very next day at Grandview Speedway in Bechtelsville, Pennsylvania, Kramer would also win the DL Motors Pennsylvania State Point Series by finishing third in the only wingless race of the 1995 season. Finishing out the year with several top-five finishes was enough for Kramer to claim his third URC Championship in 1995. Kramer also won the Jericho Triple Crown Award.

The season was everything Kramer wanted. He finally got to battle the whole season with fellow URC legend Glenn Fitzcharles driving his old Fenimore ride. Kramer edged Fitzcharles in the championship by fewer than one hundred points. Both Kramer and Fitzcharles had four wins in 1995, with the edge going to Kramer due to his consistency and many top-five finishes. Vince Gangemi and his team persevered and finally took a Ford-powered Sprint Car to the top of the URC. Kramer remembered the ups and downs of the 1995 season and his owner's willingness to give him the best car he possibly could:

> I can be a very difficult person. Vince gave me the best of everything, new tires each race or whatever it took to win. Al Rozzelle continued to squeeze more and more horsepower from the Ford. But, I am the type of person who gets frustrated very easily when mistakes happen that could have been avoided. We finished in the top five at every race this year, except Rolling Wheels, so I shouldn't complain. But like every racer, I'm always looking to

Kramer on the gas in a car some said would never win a race, let alone a championship. Kramer and owner Vince Gangemi proved the naysayers wrong in 1995, winning the URC Championship.

be a little faster. I know Vince kept track of every point we earned, but I didn't want to hear about points. If you sharpen your pencil after each race and put a plan together, everything will fall into place.

Kramer's 1995 Championship would be a significant moment in his Hall of Fame career. His championship car now rests on display at the National Sprint Car Hall of Fame as a reminder of his underdog championship. Not only was it his third URC Championship, but it would also be the last championship of his long and storied career, Although Kramer would come close several more times to winning a championship and his URC win total would continue to climb, 1995 was to be the last championship in a career that was far from over.

Kramer and the Gangemi team decided to start off the 1996 season in hopes of a second championship. While Kramer started his year with the Gangemi team, engine problems would lead him down a new path. The Ford of Gangemi's was parked in the early season as the team sorted out a new engine, and Kramer would be asked to fill in for fellow driver and businessman Fran Hogue. Kramer would eventually be hired

Kramer in a very familiar place, Victory Lane. Over his URC career, Kramer scored sixty-seven wins.

In 1996, Kramer joined the Hogue team after filling in for an injured Fran Hogue. During the season, he wrecked and damaged the car. After taking it back to his shop for repair, he was still driving the car four years later.

full-time and become a teammate to Hogue. In a 2000 interview, Kramer recalls how the relationship started:

> Back in 1996, Fran hurt his shoulder. Once he knew he'd be out a while, he asked if I wanted to fill in, which I did. Then a couple of weeks into the season, I got into a wreck and tore the car up. I told them I had everything to fix it and I'd take it home and bring it back the next week. Four years later, I still had the car.

The late entry into the 1996 season would dash all hopes for a championship run, but Kramer was able to keep his consecutive years of winning a URC feature alive by winning the very last race of the 1996 season at Elbridge, New York. Also in 1996, Kramer took his third trip to Australia to race as part of Team USA. This time, his teammates would be fellow URC competitors Fran Hogue and Greg Coverdale. The team had a great deal of success in the three-race series in the land down under as Kramer and Coverdale both won feature events and Hogue finished second twice. All three drivers drove cars owned by

From left to right are Greg Coverdale, Kramer Williamson and Fran Hogue. All three were part of Team USA during the 1996 Australia Tour.

Australian Sprint Car driver Robin Dawkins. The dominating perform-ance wowed the Aussie spectators, and the drivers were treated like royalty during their Australian tour. The trio of American drivers were interviewed and featured on TV programs, signed many autographs, and even had a parade in their honor.

Greg Coverdale remembers the trip with Kramer and the good times had overseas:

> We were putting our car together for the 1997 season and I got wind that Kramer and Fran Hogue were going to Australia. So I talked with my wife about it and she said if I wanted to go over there to go for it. I called Fran and he called Kramer to see what was going on with the trip. I had heard through John Zimmerman that they were looking for one more driver to go over there. We talked a couple times and I ended up going over there with them. I had an absolute blast. We were supposed to run five races and only ended up running three. Kramer and I both won one apiece. He was just nuts. He was such a funny guy, famous for his one-liners, and he had a bunch of them.
>
> When we got over to Australia, a guy named Robin Dawkins had three

Gambler chassis Sprint Cars all lined up for us. They had Gaerte engines and were painted up USA numbers one, two and three. One of my most treasured photos is one of all three of us sitting on our right rear tires and each driver signed the photo. It was just a good time and a lot of laughs.

All I can tell you is I went to Australia with two cameras, the little portable, disposable kind. I had one for sightseeing and my family and I had one for URC, and somehow the one for URC disappeared. I know Fran was not the one who stole it, so I know Kramer took it. I know the laughs I had with Fran and Kramer in Australia were some of the best times I ever had in racing. I mean he would get me laughing so hard your stomach hurt for two days. Those kind of good times don't come around that often. It was real fun. One night at two in the morning, I snapped a photo of him and I heard him say "son of a bitch" then the next day my camera was gone. I came home and unpacked and never saw that camera again.

With the pieced-together 1996 season behind Kramer and a successful run in Australia, things started to look brighter for the 1997 season. Kramer started the year off again driving for driver/owner Fran Hogue in the Tastykake #2 Sprint Car. Kramer's next three years with the team would be ultra-successful. In 1997, Kramer grabbed six URC feature wins and finished second in the URC Championship behind winner Sean Michael. Tim Hogue, son of driver/owner Fran Hogue, fondly

Kramer on the gas during the 1996 Australian Tour. Kramer won one race during the team's visit to the land down under.

remembers Kramer's coming on board with the team and the impact Kramer would have on the rest of his life:

> Kramer started driving for my dad in 1996. It was the first year my dad had gotten a big sponsor. We had Tastykake come on board. The third race of the year, my dad breaks his shoulder and he goes to the hospital as me and my brother stay at the track and load the car up. We had people coming over to us before we left the track to go to the hospital saying, "Hey, hope your Dad is okay, but if you need a driver I'm available." So Dad got out of the hospital and said, "Hey, we got Tastykake as a sponsor, we got to put someone in this car. Kramer's here and he won the championship the year before. Sharon is here, go find her." So we found her and Kramer and said that we need you to drive the car next week. He did, and he ran from 1996 through 1999. We finished second in the championship twice and won a bunch of races.
>
> We tried everything, changing motors, changing cars, just all kinds of crazy stuff. I just learned so much from him. I was just a freshman in college and I would go up during Christmas break and spend a week or two with him building a car. He was much more than just a driver. He was meticulous as hell. I mean about stuff that I thought was just plain old stupid.

Kramer in Victory Lane driving the #39 Tastykake car in his first year for Fran Hogue. When Hogue returned to driving, the Tastykake team became a two-car operation and Kramer drove the #2 car.

165

We were getting a car ready for the motor sports show and we were polishing stuff. He had this grinder and attached a polishing wheel to it and we had to stand outside because it left black stuff everywhere. I never will forget. I was polishing up a brand-new floor pan. It was brand-new and I polished it and polished it forever. I took it inside and showed it to him and he said, "Take it outside and do it again; it ain't good enough." I told him it was brand-new to start with, so what do you mean it's not good enough? He said, "There are swirls in it. Get them out." I was like, are you serious? But I will never forget that because it taught me how to do things the right way.

I just learned so many things like that from him, and believe it or not, racing-wise, once I started driving our car he ran into me more than anyone one the track. He was without a doubt the guy I had more contact with than anyone else on the track and I think it was because I was always just little Timmy to him. He always told me not to let the guys on the track push me around, but then he would push me around. Perhaps he was trying to teach me something. One time, I led twenty-four laps at Grandview and I had the car on the fence. With two laps to go, I start to see the nose of the pink car on the inside. I was like, no way; I'm going to the bottom to take his line. On the last lap, I go to the bottom and he went to the top and drove right around me. He did not talk to a soul in Victory Lane until he came over to me and said, "Don't ever change your line. I never would have touched you if you stayed on top. You messed up, but thanks. Don't ever do that again." That was a lesson learned.

He had so many one-liners. I think of him as one of the best ever so that part of it I never think about much because I expect everyone to think of him as one of the best. But his one-liners were what I remember most. He had a joke for everything. He used the same ones all the time and you would hear them a hundred times, but he always found someone who had never heard them before.

He is a Hall of Famer for sure and one of the greatest ever. I remember one time we went to Canada and we were racing for the championship and my dad had this motor built by a guy who was not a spectacular motor builder, probably one of the reasons we finished second in the championship, and it blew up the week before we went to Canada. We had this spare motor we called "Little Red" and Kramer did not want to go to Canada. He thought there was no point in going if we were going to run that little motor because it would simply not get the job done. This is when Autodrome Drummond was super-fast and you needed a strong motor. He flat out told my dad that he did not want to go and my dad said we have to go because of our sponsor, Tastykake. So we go up there and Kramer is not happy about going at all. After all that, Kramer sets a track record at Drummond with the little motor and he won both Canadian races as well. I think he did it out of spite, but I'm not sure. He was quite a character.

Kramer's time with the #2 Tastykake ended up to be some of the most prosperous years of his Sprint Car career. Although he never won

Although a serious competitor, Kramer was also famous for his one-liners and antics in the pits and around the track.

a championship with them, his win total was indeed impressive. In 1997, he posted six wins, tying Sean Michael for most wins that year. In 1998, he upped his win total to a URC-leading eight wins on the season and finished second again in the championship behind Curt Michael, who only won three races, but amazingly finished every single race that season, giving him the championship. In his final year driving for the Hogue team in 1999, Kramer won three URC features including the URC/ESS Challenge Series event at Rolling Wheels Speedway in New York. In his fifty-ninth URC victory, Kramer roared to the front from the twenty-first starting spot to the lead on lap eighteen. The victory capped off a successful four-year stint for the Hogue Sprint Car team. At the end of the season, Hogue informed Kramer that his son Tim was ready to try his hand at Sprint Car racing and the team simply could not afford to field another car. Always the class act, Kramer helped to pull the motor from his old ride and even helped breaking the car down before looking for a new ride in 2000.

Kramer spent his 2000 URC season driving the #33 Wayne Patterson Sprint Car out of New York for the year. In a twenty-eight-race schedule that year, Kramer came close to winning several times and posted consistent finishes, but failed to find Victory Lane until the season-ending race at Delaware International Speedway. Kramer scored his only win of 2000 in the yellow Sprinter and finished sixth in URC points for the season. His popular 2000 feature win did have historical significance, as Kramer tied Buck Buckley's career win record of sixty URC feature wins. Kramer also won the Delaware State URC Championship as well, due to his win and consistent finishes at Delaware International Speedway. The 2001 season would be a year of transition for Kramer Williamson, as he scored only one victory at Grandview Speedway in Bechtelsville, Pennsylvania, in the Ken Eldreth Sprint Car mid-season. As the start of a new millennium unfolded, so too did yet another chapter in the journey of Kramer Williamson. After the season, Kramer took a path few saw coming, which would put him back in the seat of a familiar car of a certain unique color.

8

Return of the Pink Panther

After spending most of his racing life as a hired gun, Kramer returned to his roots and for the first time in many years fielded a self-owned Sprint Car in the 2002 URC series. It really brought the driver full circle from where his racing career started. Kramer had come a long way since running his first family-owned car at Silver Spring Speedway in 1968; however, the one thing that remained a constant in his long career was his family and their constant support. The return of the pink #73 Sprint Car would be supported by family in 2002 just like it was back in 1968; only this time it would be Kramer, Sharon and their kids Kurtis and Felecia at the track working on the car week in and week out. Although his parents were now older and not able to attend most of the races, their support was still there; they remained Kramer's biggest fans and surely enjoyed seeing the #73 return to the track. During this time period, the URC resembled a traveling family with everyone looking after everyone else, so Kramer enjoyed his time with not only his family, but his URC family as well.

The first few years of once again running his own equipment and car were a big challenge. The cost of racing had escalated during the late 1990s so much that it made running a self-funded team nearly impossible. Chris Gustin of Armorboard Packing became Kramer's major sponsor for a good part of the new Pink Panther years. Chris had met Kramer some thirty years earlier through a high school friend who happened to be Kramer's cousin. Chris recalls his first meeting with Kramer and a few stories from years of racing together:

> We had always liked racing and decided we wanted to get into it. We were so green and naive. We bought an old junk Donnie Kreitz frame that he had made years ago and we hauled it over to Kramer's shop for him to look at and tell us what it needed. So Kramer looked at it and said, "Well, I know

The year 2002 marked the return of Kramer's "Pink Panther" race car. Fans were delighted to see the pink #73 on the track once again.

why Donnie Kreitz didn't win anything in this car." That was how I started to know him. We raced for about seven years and took our car to Kramer's shop to get it ready for the season and when we broke it, he would fix it up.

After my friend stopped driving, I kept the car and tried to expand the motor program a little bit. I always wanted to run a Dodge and one of my dreams was to see a Mopar in Victory Lane. I put Kramer in my car for a race at Selinsgrove and then it promptly blew up. Shortly after that, I retired from racing and got married, but I had the idea if I wanted to race again I needed more money and the only way I could do that is if I started my own company. I started my business, Armorboard, with the hopes I could go racing again.

When I started the company, I took a lot of our ideas to Kramer and he helped build many of the machines we have. The business worked out and I started to make money, so about two years later I wanted to get back into racing, but now I did not have the time to concentrate on it. That's when Armorboard started sponsoring Kramer. It was kind of ironic [that] I started this business so I could afford to go racing, and then when I got it up and going, I did not have the time to go racing, but I sponsored Kramer. I bought him a motor, paid some bills and helped anywhere we could. If things got slow at Kramer Kraft, I would have him come down and do some welding for me or make a machine or something like that. Any little project I had, he could fix. He could do anything.

One of the main reasons for Kramer's successful return to running his own Sprint Car team was the long and loyal sponsorship from Chris and Jody Gustin, owners of Armorboard Packaging.

He could be hard to talk to at first. When I first met him, I'd ask him a question and he would not answer me. Then, fifteen minutes later he would give you an answer. That was because he thought about it for that long to make sure the solution was the absolute best one there was, and I did not realize that at first. He had a different way of looking at things and a lot of the times he was correct. He did the same thing with his race cars. He was always looking for something a little bit different to make his cars go faster. He was definitely a throwback kind of racer in some ways, being able to build and work on his own equipment. But he did like to try new things on his car, sometimes to a detriment because if you know something works, just go with that, but his mind did not stop working and he was always wanting to improve things.

There are people who race and then there are racers, and Kramer and his whole family are racers. They would eat hot dogs and French fries all week to save money to put toward the car. The whole family was so dedicated to the sport. I mean, Felecia graduated from Penn State and then came down that night to watch her dad race. It's what they did and what they lived for. They were a racing family that got it done. It's not like they had a ton of money and then said let's go racing. They were racers and the whole family found a way to get what they needed to compete, and that is truly amazing.

People just liked to come down to his shop and hang around. It's weird.

Kramer in Victory Lane with the "Pink Panther." Racing since 1968, Kramer was still winning races in the new millennium, with his last victory coming in the year 2011.

People just liked to be around Kramer and be in his presence. It was always fun at the shop and there were always people stopping by. You know, in a way, he was still a fifteen-year-old boy. He had the same jokes he would tell you over and over and you loved him for that. He made a lot of friends and had a lot of people who liked him. I loved walking around with him. You could meet darn near everybody. Going to the races with Kramer was indeed special. He knew everyone and used to joke by saying, "I could never cheat on Sharon. Everyone knows me." We walked by the gate at Daytona and someone said to Jeff Gordon, "Hey, Kramer Williamson is out here," and Jeff said, "Oh, yeah, tell him to come on in." We were at Williams Grove and Tony Stewart came right up and started a conversation with him. The Blaneys were good friends, and the list goes on and on.

He was such a nice guy, but a funny story about Kramer is the only pit fight I ever got into was with Kramer Williamson up in New York. Some guy thought we put his car in the wall and we did not even come close to his car. He comes flying in the pits and runs into Kramer's car and it was on. I mean a full-on brawl. After it was all said and done, I said to myself, "How in the hell did I just get into a pit fight with Kramer Williamson? I mean, everyone likes Kramer—he doesn't have any enemies." I will remember him as someone everyone just wanted to be around and be in his company.

Chris and his sponsorship rode with Kramer on his car until his passing in 2013. An almost unheard-of seventeen-plus years of sponsoring one single driver shows the friendship and mutual respect shared between Chris and Kramer during the twilight of Kramer's career.

While the Armorboard sponsorship certainly helped, 2002 would be a tough first season back for car owner and driver as Kramer Williamson struggled to find the form that had brought him so many victories and championships in years past. The struggle continued through the 2003 and 2004 seasons as well. Although Kramer posted no wins during those seasons, he did finish fifth in the URC point standings at the end of the 2004 season. Some were asking if Kramer had lost the feel for these new-style Sprint Cars. Gone were the tiny wings of the past. The URC Sprinters of the new millennium had larger wings and front wings on them than any other cars before. Had Kramer simply not been able to adapt to these new cars? Many were asking if it was time for the fifty-five-year-old to driver hang up the helmet and walk away from the sport he loved so dearly, but Kramer was far from done and had many more wins left to claim.

In 2005, Kramer got back on track, winning two races that year at Delaware International Speedway and at Grandview Speedway. Delaware

International Speedway owner and promoter Charlie Cathell remembers Kramer's impact not only on the track, but on the fans with that pink car.

> Kramer was probably one of the URC's biggest stars. He was a people person. He knew how to get along with a crowd. When he was running for Tastykake, he would give out pies and snacks to everyone. I think the color of his car attracted a lot of kids and females to visit with him and once you met him you were an instant fan. You could look in the stands on a night URC was there and half of the crowd was dressed in pink. I know he loved Delmar; it was one of his favorite race tracks. I know it was a long tow for him, but he always did well at our track. He told me he looked forward to coming here [more] than any other race track he went to. He was always in the mix in the front. I used to say the Pink Panther was always nipping at you. His legacy and driving that pink race car will live on forever. He was so good when the track got slick and hard. He was such a natural and with the color of his car you just could not help but watch him. Your eye was just drawn to that car and most of the time it was at the front or headed there. He was old school when it comes to drivers. The only thing most people do in the garage now is clean the clay off the car. He built his stuff from scratch and did not just assemble it like a lot of people do. His whole family was involved in everything with the operation of the race team, from setting the car up to selling T-shirts behind the grandstands. One of the biggest complaints I hear from car owners today is that they can't get anyone to help them prepare the car through the week and there is no one to go and help at the track. That was not the case with Kramer. He always had his family there to help with the car and they loved it. He always got the job done and I had a lot of respect for him. Kramer and his family were always welcome at our speedway; he was a class act.

His efforts in the 2005 season were enough to garner a fifth-place finish in the URC points that year and earn the Delaware URC State Championship. Kramer also finished fifth in the car owner points and enjoyed being competitive again in his own equipment and team. The 2006 season was a rare winless season by the veteran driver, who came close to winning on so many occasions. His consistency helped him place fifth in URC points for a second consecutive year as he maintained his top-five status in the ever-changing URC.

In one of his most successful years running his own #73 Pink Panther Sprint Car, Kramer entered the 2007 season in what would become known as one of the most competitive seasons in URC history. Twenty different drivers won URC races throughout the long 2007 season. Kramer would win three features during the year, one at his old stomping grounds, Hagerstown, Maryland, and the other two at Delaware

Pictured here at one of the tracks where Kramer started his career, Williams Grove, Kramer still had what it took to win races some forty-plus years after his first race. In 2007, Kramer won three races and finished fourth in URC points.

International Speedway, where he was always a threat to win. His win total was the same as 2007 URC Champion Curt Michael, who won three races as well. After a hard-fought year, Kramer finished fourth in the URC Points Championship and won the URC Pennsylvania Points Championship, silencing critics who said he should retire and hang up his helmet. The Pink Panther was back in a big way, and the legend was just simply adding to his résumé of impressive stats.

The year 2008 will always be remembered as a highlight in Kramer's career, as he would finally be inducted into the National Sprint Car Hall of Fame in Knoxville, Iowa. The honor is the highlight of any successful racer's career and definitely puts him in rare air amongst the greatest to ever strap in and drive a Sprint Car. The Hall of Fame Class of 2008 included his old nemesis from the URC, Glenn Fitzcharles, as well. Sharon remembers Kramer's excitement when he got the call to be inducted: "He was thrilled! A TV station came and did an interview with him and he was just super excited and honored. We made the trip out and he actually brought the car along to race as well. We did not do well that night, but it was a great trip." The whole family, as well as old friends including Bob Trostle, made it out to the ceremony. The unique thing about Kramer that made him stand out from the other inductees in 2008 was the fact he was still actively racing and winning some forty-plus years after making his first start in a full-sized race car.

Daughter Felecia recalls her dad's pride in being inducted into the Hall of Fame and what made him even more proud than any award he could receive.

> There were a lot of different things that Dad was very proud of, but he was
> a very humble guy. After his accident, I thought about all the stuff he had

In 2008 Kramer rightfully took his place among the greatest ever to drive a Sprint Car. The Williamson family—from left to right, Kurtis, Kramer, Sharon and Felecia—attend Kramer's induction into the National Sprint Car Hall of Fame.

accomplished and why he did not have a bigger head with all of his wins and successes, but he didn't, and he kept Mom, Kurt and me very grounded. The Hall of Fame in his mind was a huge honor and accomplishment, but more important to him than that was the fact that his family was always involved and together during his career. Racing was not just a hobby, it was what we did together, and he was very proud that we all did it together. I remember when I was graduating from Penn State, I was so worried he wouldn't come, but he proudly watched me get my college degree up in University Park, Pennsylvania, and we then rushed over to race at Selinsgrove Speedway for the night. I didn't even have time to take my graduation gown off or my heels, so [I] ran across the track to rush to get heat in the motors! It ended up raining out, but we always went to the races together. Another time was about a month before his accident. We started a tradition to go to Utica Rome Speedway up in New York to race with the ESS over the 4th of July since Kurt could be at home from his NASCAR schedule. It was a Sunday race and I had to go to Maine for work and could not go. Dad just said, "Nope, we're not going. If Felecia can't go, we're not going to race." We all went or we didn't go, that's just how he was.

Some of Kramer's impressive statistics that put him in the National Sprint Car Hall of Fame included: 1968 Rookie of the Year, Silver Spring Speedway; 1969 Silver Spring Super Sportsman Track Champion; 1971 Rookie of the Year at Williams Grove Speedway, Port Royal and Susquehanna Speedways; 1975, won four of seven races on All Star Circuit; 1977 Florida Winter Nationals Champion; 1976 and 1978 Track Champion at Williams Grove Speedway; 1978 Track Champion at Selinsgrove; 1976 and 1978 KARS Champion; 1978 Summer KARS Summer Nationals Champion; 1978 Williams Grove Speedway National Open Winner; 1991 URC Champion and URC Triple Crown Champion; 1992 URC Champion; 1993 Runner-up URC Points (six wins); 1995 URC Champion and URC Triple Crown Champion; 1997 Runner-up URC Points (six wins); 1998 Runner-up URC Points (8 wins); 2000 Delaware State URC Champion; 2005 URC Delaware State URC Champion; raced in Australia three times (1983, 1986, and 1996), winning twice. Kramer had over one hundred and fifty feature wins in his long career.

The National Sprint Car Hall of Fame was not the only Hall of Fame he was inducted into. Over his career he was also inducted into the York County Racing Hall of Fame as a Present Driver Honoree in 1994; United Racing Company Hall of Fame in 2010; Central Pennsylvania Sports Hall of Fame in 2011; the Auto Racing Club of Hagerstown Hall of Fame in 2015; and the Eastern Motorsports Press Association Hall of Fame in January of 2017.

One would think that with a résumé as prestigious as Kramer's, coupled with his induction into the National Sprint Car Hall of Fame, he might think about hanging up his helmet. Definitely not the case with Kramer; still having fun and still competitive, Kramer continued to do what he loved: race. He was often quoted as saying, "The goal is to win races and have fun; if you aren't having fun then it's time to quit." In fact, after every night's race Kramer would always turn to his family and utter the same question: "Well, did we have fun tonight?" The answer was always yes! The Williamsons continued to do the only thing they knew: race and enjoy their time together as a family. Sure, the victories started to come fewer and farther in between, but the racing near the end of Kramer's career was just as fun as it always had been. Nothing could stop Kramer from racing, not even the threat of jail time in 2009, as Sharon remembers:

> Kramer was going to drive Tom Buch's car at Charlotte for the World Finals. It was Kramer, me and the family dogs, otherwise referred to as "the kids" first trip in the new toterhome. We were heading to Kurt's place in North Carolina and Felecia was meeting us there. Well, a week before the race [Kramer] got a letter to report for jury duty. Well, there was no way he was going to miss a race. Turns out we headed for North Carolina and called the guy on our way. He said there was no way you could get out of jury duty unless you are sick and have a doctor's excuse. So we went to the care center in the Charlotte area with Kramer claiming he had a sore throat. Well, it ended up he really did have strep throat, so he got his note to be excused from jury duty. The guy from jury duty actually threatened Kramer that he would go to jail if he did not show up. I think that was one time in Kramer's life that he was scared. I guess you could say thank goodness for that throat infection.

The years of watching Kramer race had a huge influence on his son Kurtis. Helping on his dad's car almost since he could hold a wrench, Kurt learned from doing, and there was always plenty to do in the garage of Kramer Williamson. Working as a shock specialist on the NASCAR circuit at the time, Kurtis would get home every chance he could to help with the race car. Kurt remembers growing up working on his dad's cars and the influence Kramer had on his career: "I remember working on the Gangemi car as a kid. I tightened bolts, scraped mud off the car and even changed some gears. I really stepped forward when our crew chief left in the middle of the year. The time I remember most was at Rolling Wheels Speedway. Dad got out of the car and just said, 'Everything sucked and do what you want to the car.' He was just really frustrated because I think we were in the B-main. From then on, I can remember working on the cars more and more."

Kramer even had a guiding hand in Kurt's career choice and his decision to head south and work for some of NASCAR's biggest teams, and eventually to start his own business with a familiar name, Kramer Kraft.

> At the time when I was in college at Penn State Berks, and shocks started to become a real big deal in dirt racing. The technology just took off in dirt racing around 2001 and Dad said Penske is right by you. I really just wanted to go work there so I could learn about the shocks so Dad could get an advantage in his car with them. I was not really thinking it would lead to a whole career. I basically went into Penske and was sweeping the floor and taking out the trash. Then they started to let me do some pre-assembly, and Dave Reedy, who was a local dirt track guy that worked at Penske, kind of took me under his wing, and one day they gave me a shock to take apart and put together. I asked a lot of questions and learned a lot. I was working for Penske doing the NASCAR thing and was down at Dover International Speedway and got some job offers, but I really did not want to go because I wanted to stay in Pennsylvania and race Sprint Cars with my dad. But Dad decided and told me that you need to go, it's a great opportunity. He said it will suck with you gone and we will miss you, but it's a great way to better yourself. He always had our best interest in mind.

The racing gene definitely did not skip a generation, and Kurtis inherited his dad's inquisitive mind and mechanical ability. Kramer was always looking to outsmart the competition and gain some sort of edge, a trait passed down from dad to son. Kurt explains just how much his dad enjoyed finding ways to go faster:

> He loved racing and had a deep passion for it. I believe he had more of a passion for building race cars more so than driving them. I think he was more interested in building something to outsmart someone than to out-race them. He always told me you got to outsmart them, that's how you beat them. He would be at the shop through the week and just ask me, "What about this? What about that?" There was like a year or two that he did not win any races and the reason why was because he decided we were going to have fun and experimented with a bunch of different things. We tried everything. He had all kinds of weird stuff on his cars around that time. He would put something illegal in plain sight to draw other competitors' attention away from the stuff he was really wanting to try and get away with. He liked to get into their heads. A lot of times it bit us in the butt; however, it was fun trying different stuff out. The car my mom has now as the show car was a split bar car. It was supposed to be the latest and greatest, but we never got it hooked up right. I think about it to this day and

what we could have done to make that car faster and I still have a few ideas what to do to make it work.

Before Kurt started Kramer Kraft, he would get garage passes for the family for the spring and fall Dover races every year when he started working with NASCAR. Even though Kramer wasn't racing himself, he loved walking around the garage down at Dover and talking to everyone he knew, including Jeff Gordon, Tony Stewart, and Dave Blaney, and even meeting new friends. One year, Kurt even got a spare radio for Kramer to listen to the race. Kurt gave Kramer specific instructions on which buttons he could touch and which ones he couldn't touch. After the race, Kurt told Sharon and Felecia about how Kramer had hit the button and the crew chief couldn't communicate with the driver. Whoops! The next race, Kurt did the same thing by getting an extra radio for Kramer, but Kurt had to make sure to say, "Whatever you do, don't hit this button!!" Fun times like this were very common for the Williamson family, always enjoying their time together.

Sharing his dad's passion for racing led Kurt to start Kramer Kraft, borrowing the name from his dad's famous race shop. Today's Kramer Kraft focuses on shocks for the Camping World Truck Series, ARCA, and the Xfinity Series. The skills learned watching his father's Sprint Car on the track transfer directly to his job today, as Kurtis explains:

> Watching the cars on the track now and adjusting the shocks to fit what the car is doing is one of my better skills, and I learned that from watching Dad run his Sprint Car and the car's attitude as it went around the corners. I look for the attitude of the car and how it rolls. Like this year at Eldora, I watched Ken Schrader qualify and the way his truck handled in the corners. Then, I will take pictures with my phone and look at how the car is sitting in certain places. Then, I give the team some suggestions and Ken tells me how the car is handling and reacting on the track. We will make the proper adjustments. Kenny was having a good race at Eldora and was running well until the shock mounts broke off the frame because the track was so rough. At first, I was nervous one of my shocks came apart, but after the race we found the broken mount. It was kind of neat to be at Eldora near the same time of year that my dad won back in the day in the Pink Panther. I can trace back all my skills directly to Dad's racing and it's neat to be able to use them at this level.

Kurtis made the long drives back to Pennsylvania as often as he could as his father continued to do what he loved. In the 2010 season, Kramer was enjoying yet another resurgence in his racing career and was solidly in the top ten in URC points. After a strong second-place finish at his favorite Delaware International Speedway, it was off to Georgetown for yet another race. Heading into turn one at full speed, Kramer's car suffered a steering malfunction, sending Kramer into a row of trees well beyond the track. Even when things went terribly wrong, Kramer always remained calm and in control. Sharon remembers just how calm he was that night at Georgetown Speedway:

> Kramer's power steering went out going into turn one and he spun and backed the car into the woods. His car got wedged between two trees so they were having a hard time getting him out of the car. Of course, he didn't want them to just bang and pound his car, so he was standing in the seat of the car telling them what bolts to take off so they could get him out of the car. Felecia and I were in the fourth turn because we had no idea what was going on. I kept giving the officials a hard time because I needed to know if he was okay. I told them I didn't believe them because he wasn't out of the car. Bob Miller finally gave Kramer his official's radio so he could talk to us and let us know he was fine.

Felecia remembers her dad coming over the radio, saying, "Tell those blondes to relax, I'm fine. I'll see them soon."

Kramer's last win would come on April 30, 2011, at Delaware International Speedway, a track where he was dominant throughout his long career. From left to right in Victory Lane are Sharon, Kramer and Felecia Williamson.

181

Staying calm in times of chaos is one of the traits of a great champion, and despite the parts failure that caused the crash, Kramer continued throughout the season posting strong finishes and concentrating on having fun and experimenting with his car. In the 2011 URC season, Kramer again started off strong. When the URC headed back to Delaware International Speedway on April 30, 2011, Kramer for the last time in his forty-plus-year career would win a Sprint Car feature. The win was not only the last of his long, successful career, but it was also his sixty-seventh URC win. In Victory Lane, Sharon and Felecia were there to enjoy the moment and take in the applause from the capacity crowd at Delaware International Speedway. It was fitting that Kramer's last win would come at one of his very favorite tracks, a speedway he had dominated since the 1980s in a Sprint Car.

When traveling to Delaware and other URC destinations late in

The Williamson family poses for a photograph during the 2011 season before Kramer heads out to the track. From left to right are Kramer, Felecia, Kurtis and Sharon Williamson.

his career, Kramer often relied on the help of his extended family. One person who was there through thick and thin was neighbor and friend Cliffy Irvin, who lived right down the street from Kramer. Cliffy describes his duties on the team and thoughts on his boss and friend, Kramer:

> I helped Kramer for almost twenty years. I did a lot of maintenance on the car and would clean it up the next day after the team got back late at night. He was a fun guy and liked to get under people's skin in a good way. Kramer was always willing to help someone and often went out of his way to do that. I used to help him weld the frames together, make front axles and just about everything else you could think of. I learned a lot from Kramer and owe a lot to him.

It took a village to keep the Pink Panther running, and everyone played a part on the team and within the family. Everyone, from those at the track to those behind the scenes, enjoyed the celebration of that hard-fought win in 2011. A racer never knows when the last win will come, and Kramer's victory was enjoyed to its fullest and etched in the minds of those who witnessed it forever. Now, not only had Kramer raced for over forty years, but over forty years had passed between his first win and his last victory, an incredible span of time to race, let alone remain competitive and win. Interestingly, both his first and last wins came in family-owned #73 Pink Panther Sprint Cars.

9

The Final Lap
of the Pink Panther

After his win in 2011, Kramer continued to race with the URC regularly. In a 2012 interview with Mike Calla, it was easy to see the fire was still burning bright in the Sprint Car veteran. Kramer commented on his age and his race plans: "My body will tell me when it's time to stop. We do plan to run the entire URC season even though I would like more race dates on the schedule. When you get to this stage of my career, you want to race every possible weekend." Always thinking about the fans and how good of a show URC put on was also important to Kramer, as was exemplified by his comments on the debated double file restarts: "I think it will be exciting and something different for me. Double file restarts will help. I get stronger as the race goes on. I'm glad URC is trying it and if it makes the racing better for the fans, then we have to do it after all, it's all about the fans." If those comments were not enough to convince you that the sixty-two-year-old's competiveness was still strong, then maybe his comment about URC's offering higher-paying events to attract more competition will send a message that he was not a field-filler, but came to the track to win: "Good, bring them on. I want to kick their butts. I have always believed that if you race with good drivers, you'll be a good driver. I believe it's my way to get better. I remember beating Fred Rahmer at the Grove one night driving Fran Hogue's car, and it was so sweet, and I want to do more of that."

Kramer raced his way through 2012 and early 2013, still having fun and still a fan favorite, before tragedy struck on the night of August 3, 2013. Kramer's wife Sharon describes the events of that fateful night at Lincoln Speedway and the days following:

Sharon Williamson would always stand in front of Kramer's car before he headed out to the track. Kramer would give her a wink before being pushed out for the night's events.

The night before at Williams Grove Speedway on August 2, there were all kinds of photographers and media hanging out at the car. Lots of photos were being taken. I said to Felecia that it's like the paparazzi is hanging out here tonight. We actually had a family picture taken that night, but no one ever thought it would be our last photo all together as a family.

Kramer was upset with the way his newest-built Kramer Kraft car handled Friday night at Williams Grove, so when he got back to the shop on Friday night, he decided that he was going to run his backup car. The car was a split bar car that he was playing around with, because trying new things is what Kramer did. Unfortunately, it did not handle like he wanted and this was not the weekend to try to get a new car to handle. So Kramer, Max Hauck and Kurt worked late getting the backup car ready for Saturday night racing at Lincoln Speedway.

We left for the races Saturday in the totter. Felecia, Kurt's friend, me and "the kids" all piled in the totter and headed to Lincoln. "The kids" were Kramer's beloved Yorkshire terrier dogs named Kozmo and Summer that traveled with them everywhere. Kurt was at Pocono with NASCAR, so he was driving down after the race and meeting us at the racetrack.

Kramer was in the first heat race. We had just come in from the warm-ups and all of a sudden it was like rush, rush, let's get the first heat out. I remember one of Kramer's ear pieces to his radio was missing. The ear

Kramer had fun and loved what he did all the way right up until the end, as evidenced in one of their last family photographs. Left to right: Felecia, Kramer, Kurtis and Sharon are all smiles enjoying family and a night of racing.

piece was not that old and he had it molded for his ears when we were in North Carolina over the winter months. He always hated his radios. He said you can barely hear anything anyway. I jokingly said to him while he was getting into the car, when you get in from the heat race, we are going into the totter and you are taking your uniform off. I was assuming the ear mold fell down into his uniform while he was putting it on. He kind of laughed it off, like sure.

Felecia did her usual safety routine, making her daddy show her that the steering wheel was on tight. She gave him a fist bump and Kramer always winked back at her. Kurt gave him a fist bump and Kramer was off to run what was his last race.

It was the first heat. Kramer was running the outside, which he rarely runs, to make a pass. On the fourth lap of the heat race, in turns one and two, Kramer had a great run and ran up and over the tire of a car he was passing and that started the fatal flip. Kramer was definitely on a mission as he had the Pink Panther hooked up. He was fast and going to the front on his very last lap of racing.

I remember Felecia screaming and running down to the accident scene (like she always does when her dad crashed). I stayed on top of the trailer where we were watching the race. I've learned over the years to just stay put, and I will be able to see him get out of the car, except on this night I didn't see him get out. I felt in my heart something was not right. I started walking to the first and second turn and then ran. I remember Felecia kept screaming "Daddy" and I knew it was bad. The track crew would not let us near the car. It seemed like eternity waiting for them to get Kramer out of the car. When I heard them calling in the Life Flight, I knew it wasn't good.

As they were working on getting Kramer out of the car, they told me to go to the hospital so I would be there when he got there. Julie Grasso, J.J. Grasso's wife, drove Felecia and me to the York Hospital.

I remember sitting in the emergency room. We actually beat the helicopter there, but of course, why wouldn't we? A race car driver's wife drove us there. I remember sitting there and all of a sudden a hospital worker came and said, "Are you the family of (she said some really strange name)?" I said, "No, never heard of that name before." Then she said, "Oh, it's the guy that was just flown in from the racetrack." I actually got a big smile on my face thinking, Kramer is okay. He is playing his name games on them. Anyone that knows Kramer knew when you asked him his name, he would blurt out George Bush, Bill Clinton or some kind of crazy name. So when she said that I figured he was okay. I could finally breathe. After the helicopter got there they took us up to the second floor. They rushed him into an exploratory surgery to see if there was any internal bleeding. When we finally saw Kramer, I knew he was far from being okay. He was not conscious and very swollen from the trauma. After the kids and I kissed him and told him we loved him, we went back in the waiting area for what seemed like forever. We had many friends there with us. The newspaper media were patiently waiting for any information, but the hospital would not release any information without our permission. The hospital staff kept asking us if we wanted to release a statement and said many people, fans included, were calling the hospital to see how Kramer was doing.

When the trauma surgeon finally came and took us to a separate room to speak with us, I will never forget the words she said to me. As I sat there the trauma surgeon said to me, "I'm so sorry, Mrs. Williamson, but there is not much we can do for your husband. Your husband was without oxygen for twenty minutes." Those were the exact words. At that time, I realized this was really, really, not good and she said they were doing all they could. She explained that there was no internal injuries or bleeding and Kramer did not have one broken bone in his entire body. She said as soon as they got Kramer to his room in Trauma Surgical ICU that we could go be with him. There were lots of friends and fans there waiting for us. It seemed like it took forever. When we finally got to see Kramer, he was ventilated, with all kinds of tubes and wires in him. Kramer's face and body were very much swollen. There was even an indentation at the side of Kramer's head where his glasses were. I never left Kramer's side, only to go tell our friends that there was not much they could do and they should go home and when they would take him out for testing his brain function. I remember seeing tears run down the side of his face and I knew in my heart he was crying.

I remember them taking him to CTA to assess brain perfusion. They needed to perform an apnea test of Kramer's brain. They explained to Kurt, Felecia and I that he probably would code and his heart would stop when they ran his test. They surely didn't know Kramer well ... he was strong as an ox, so to speak. He didn't code and his heart didn't stop. After the first test, the results came back that they were ninety percent sure that he had no brain function. I told them that wasn't good enough. The kids and I, making the decisions together, told the doctors that ninety percent was not good enough. I believed in miracles and that unless he was one hundred percent brain dead, I was not going to unhook any life support. They ran that same test four times and Kramer never coded. The last time they ran it, the doctors took Kurt, Felecia and me and showed us his brain function and explained all the medical terms. In layman's terms, Kramer was one hundred percent brain dead.

I never dreamed that Kramer would lose his life in a racing tragedy. We were all with Kramer when he passed on that Sunday afternoon, August 4, 2013.

The next few days are all kind of a blur for me. We went to see Travis Finkenbinder, owner of Rothermel Funeral Home in our hometown of Palmyra, Pennsylvania. We all sat down, and Travis got the information he needed. When it came to the part of picking out a casket, we all decided what we wanted. When Travis asked us what color we wanted, I think he about crapped his pants when we said, "Pink!" Well, after a lot of chatter, all Travis said was, "I will see what I can do."

Kramer was actually buried in a pink casket. Bruce Rambler, the friend who painted Kramer's race cars, just happened to have some pink paint left over from the last paint job he did for Kramer. So the casket was pink, and then Bruce and Brian Boyer (our lettering designer) decided that they needed to put decals on to match the race car. It was perfect. I'm sure Kramer was very proud of that; his casket matched his legendary Pink Panther race car.

When we decided on visitation. We knew there would be a lot of people, but never imagined how many. We had the Pink Panther Sprint Car on display at the funeral home. The viewing was scheduled from 5:00 p.m. to 9:00 p.m. The last person went through the line to visit Kramer at 12:45 a.m. Travis kept telling us that we could cut it off anytime. Kurt, Felecia and I were exhausted, but there was no way we were leaving until the last person went through the line. The line was so long, in fact, that Travis went to a local pizza shop and purchased pizzas to feed people who had been waiting in line for hours. He set up a table outside by the Pink Panther we had on display and people were able to eat, have some cookies, chat with others about Kramer, and still wait in line. There were people waiting in line for four hours and we had people who traveled from far away. On Thursday, the day of the services, we were supposed to start at 9:00 a.m. Travis came to our home and picked us up at 8:30 a.m., telling us there were already people in line. Services were to start at 11:00 a.m. The last person that went through the line was at 11:50 a.m. Travis told us this was the biggest funeral he had ever had.

The funeral procession was led by a street-legal Sprint Car sporting a #73 on the wing. We went past our home, where we had the race car on display out in the front yard. Neighbors and fans surrounded the car in the front yard with flowers.

A week after Kramer's accident, when he was supposed to be racing at Selinsgrove Speedway, we ended up having a memorial race for Kramer. A huge thank-you to Charlie Paige and Steve Inch for everything they did that week after Kramer's accident. It was fitting to have seventy-three pink balloons released into the air after Steve gave a nice speech about all of Kramer's accomplishments in his career. Fans were encouraged to wear pink and it looked like a sea of pink, which was really awesome to see all the support from the fans.

Felecia and I continue to go to races on a regular basis. Kurt is busy with his Kramer Kraft business in North Carolina, keeping the Kramer Kraft name going on. A lot of people ask how we can go to the races. It's simply all we ever did. Kramer would want us to continue going. People [are always] coming up and telling us stories about how they met Kramer or how they watched Kramer when they were little. I guess you could say I learn something about Kramer every time someone tells me their story of how they got to know Kramer. It is sure rewarding, and yes, I sometimes cry when people tell me their story, but it's a good cry. Kramer was respected and loved by more people than you would ever know. Selinsgrove continues to have a Kramer Williamson memorial race each year, now called the Kramer Cup. Selinsgrove Ford has a Kramer Cup parade, the same day as the race at the track, where the race cars are on display at the dealership all day and then they drive the Sprint Cars as well as Late Models and Pro Stocks down Main Street in Selinsgrove to the racetrack. Of course, the Pink Panther is always the lead car.

I guess in all the years with Kramer, to me, Kurt and Felecia, he was just Kramer or Dad. We didn't realize how many people's lives he touched or how many people had so much respect and love for him.

Over the course of the next few races after Kramer's passing, the skies would usually turn pink. Social media from one track posted that Kramer was there watching the race. There are many pink skies and every time, people to this day say it's a Kramer Sky. Kramer died doing what he loved, RACING!

The racing world had lost a giant. Kramer Williamson passed away on Sunday, August 4, 2013, at the age of sixty-three, one day after his accident at Lincoln Speedway. Word spread around in the close-knit racing community like wildfire, and family, friends and fans were stunned at the loss of the Sprint Car legend. It was a dark time for Sprint Car racing during the summer of 2013. Earlier in the year, on June 12, 2013, Jason Leffler lost his life in a Sprint Car accident at Bridgeport Speedway when his car suffered a front suspension failure. On August

5, 2013, NASCAR star and avid Sprint Car fan and driver Tony Stewart broke his tibia and fibula in his right leg after crashing a Sprint Car while leading a race at Iowa Speedway. Sprint Car racing is a tough game and the players all know the risks, but that never makes the loss easier. Tributes poured in from all over the United States as word spread on Kramer's passing, and unfortunately, so did false rumors on social media. Rumors swirled on Kramer's cause of death and continue to this day. An important issue to his wife Sharon is getting the facts straight about what happened. Sharon knows well the risk involved in her husband's chosen career and places no blame on any person because we all know how dangerous racing is, and as racers, they accept that. However, to dispel rumors, Sharon speaks frankly on the reason behind her husband's death and some improvements that she hopes could save other racers in the future:

> There are lots of rumors out there saying the cage crushed and that the wing mounts went through his helmet. Well, let me just clarify. The cage did what it was supposed to do. The only reason the cage appeared crushed down is when they used the jaws of life to cut Kramer out, it bent the cage downward. Kramer's helmet had a scratch on it. He had rocks come in and put bigger dents in his helmet than the scratch from the accident. Kramer died because he was not administered oxygen.
>
> I think the racers now are totally prepared and have the best safety equipment, but I think we now need to concentrate on getting emergency responders at all tracks fully trained for racing type emergencies. This is my hope. If by me getting my story out there saves just one racer, it will be well worth my effort.

As family, friends and fans grieved and honored Kramer Williamson over the weeks and months following the accident, many reflected on the legacy of one of Sprint Car racing's best and most lovable stars. While many questioned why a sixty-three-year-old was still racing Sprint Cars in the first place, friend and competitor Lynn Paxton puts it all in perspective from the mind of a racer:

> He was just such a natural. Everybody loved him to drive for them because he was so good at a lot of different things. His love for the sport caused him to race for forty-five years. He probably stuck around for longer than he should have, but he loved what he was doing. I had so many people say after his accident, "Well, isn't that a shame?" I said, "Yeah, it is, but how many people get to do exactly what they love right up until the very end?" Fred Rahmer asked me a year or two before he retired. He said, "Paxton, you walked away. When do you know it's time to retire from racing?" And I said let me tell ya, when you are at the races and your mind is somewhere else,

that's when it's time to retire. When you're at the races and your mind is on your kid's ball game or something else, then it's time to go. He thought that was a very good answer. Smokey Snellbaker used to come by and give me a bunch of excuses why he was still racing and one day I said, "Smokey, do you enjoy it?" And he said yes. I said great, then keep doing it, age has nothing to do with it as long as you're still having fun. Kramer had more fun than any other person I can think of and he did what he wanted until the day he passed.

Longtime promoter and friend Alan Kretzer remembers Kramer by the legacy of excellence he established during the early part of his career in central Pennsylvania with his winning ways:

> I think people will remember Kramer by the measure of excellence he established in his career. He was always a winner and covered all aspects of the racing. He started off driving as a kid. He was a champion wherever he went. He won big races. He built his own cars, which is really unusual. He was always a lot of fun and I enjoyed how we became closer as life went on. I think he certainly has to be considered one of the best.

Fellow National Sprint Car Hall of Fame member Doug Wolfgang has many fond memories of Kramer, but mostly remembers the personal side of him:

> The older guys like me will remember him in the Pink Panther in the early seventies when he was so dominant in that car and for being a cut-up guy of a really good nature. He was never a villain at the race track or some badass you did not want to be around. I will remember him as being my friend and I don't say that lightly because I can remember my dad telling me when I was younger, "Take care of your friends, pal." I asked my dad why and he said, "Because when you get old like me, you realize you only had about three to five good friends your whole life." So when I say I remember him as my friend, I say that with the utmost respect because he truly was a great friend.

Much like Doug Wolfgang, Tim Hamilton, fellow racer and son of car owner Al Hamilton, remembers the qualities Kramer had that are often lost in the heat of competition and not mentioned because of the driven nature of the sport:

> I think in retrospect you can talk about numerical accomplishments and all types of things and you can win every race, but if you have not been kind to people and appreciative, it's all for naught and I think those are attributes Kramer carried throughout his career. Kramer was appreciated and liked by lots of people because he was just that kind of guy. That is an important legacy and I think it's easy to lose sight of that in racing. We can become so driven in racing we tend to forget about things like that.

A common theme that runs through everyone's fond memories of Kramer was his kindness to others and his willingness to help when needed. Perhaps more than his sixty-seven URC wins or even his seventy-seven central Pennsylvania Sprint Car wins, it will be Kramer's personality rather than his statistics that people will remember the most, a true testament to the kind of person he was and how he lived his life. Perhaps the kind way he treated others came from his Masonic brotherhood. Kramer was a Mason and member of Brownstone Lodge #666 F. & A.M. in Hershey, Pennsylvania, and the Harrisburg, Pennsylvania, Consistory. It seemed everyone remembered Kramer in some different way, but one thing remained consistent—all the memories were good ones. Kramer left a legacy worthy for all of us to aspire to.

With so many Sprint Car drivers from all over the country, being called a legend in the sport by your peers is certainly an honor, and Kramer was indeed a legend by every definition of the word. Former URC President John Zimmerman has his opinion on where Kramer stands in Sprint Car history:

> I think he is a legend in our sport. That's how I remember him. When you're listing the greatest of the greatest Sprint Car drivers, and there are an awful lot of them, he is right up there. In my opinion, the top three Sprint Car drivers ever are Tommy Hinnershitz, A.J. Foyt and Steve Kinser, and I would not be afraid to put Kramer in the top twenty Sprint Car drivers ever. He won in Pennsylvania when Mitch Smith, Lynn Paxton, Jan Opperman, Kenny Weld and many others were in their prime. I don't know if there was ever a tougher time to win than during that time period.

The racing community is made up of some fine people, and there is often no better evidence of that than when an unfortunate tragedy happens to one of their own. Tracks that Kramer frequented announced they would collect donations in the weeks' races following Kramer's death to benefit the Williamson family. Grandview Speedway also took up a collection to benefit the Williamson family. Delaware International Speedway and New Egypt Speedway both hosted "Think Pink"–themed races. The stands at many of the tracks where Kramer raced were filled with fans wearing Kramer's trademark color, pink, for the weeks to come, and to this day, when you attend a Sprint Car race, you are sure to find someone in the crowd wearing a T-shirt with Kramer Williamson's name on it and a Pink Sprint Car.

Kramer Williamson was survived by his wife Sharon, daughter Felecia, son Kurt, and brother George. As the family grieved for the loss of Kramer, they would celebrate his life in the only way they knew. As tributes and memorials poured in from across the country, the Williamson family did as Kramer would have wanted: they went to the races.

Less than a week after his passing, Selinsgrove Speedway, the same speedway that played such an important role in Kramer's career, hosted the URC and held the Kramer Williamson Memorial Race. With a huge crowd in attendance, Sharon, Felecia and Kurt fired up the Pink Panther Sprint Car and Kurt drove it to pace the field during a few laps before the drop of the green flag for the URC feature event. With the grandstands filled with rows of people dressed in pink, the crowd paid homage to Kramer Williamson and stood as the #73 passed by, leading the field to the green flag.

As the pink #73 pulled off the track, the URC Sprints came to life and the race was on to see who would win the Kramer Williamson Memorial Race. Dave Mazy, Randy West, and Davie Franek battled in the early laps for the race lead as J.J. Grasso marched through the field from his twelfth-place starting position. J.J. Grasso used both the high and low lines to continue his march to the front, and on lap seventeen he made the winning pass for the lead. Several caution flags would wave later in the race, causing the leader to think about the emotional victory that could be his: "I kind of broke down during that caution a little bit. It's just very emotional and I thought, isn't this thing ever going to end? I just wanted to get this thing in Victory Lane. He [Kramer] was here with us tonight. The tires were burned off of this sucker. Kramer was here with us the last time and I wish he was here tonight." Crossing under a pink and black checkered flag, Grasso claimed victory in the annual running of the Kramer Williamson Memorial Race, now named the Kramer Cup.

It seemed like Kramer Williamson had one more race to win—J.J. Grasso's winning #25 Ken Eldreth race car was none other than a Kramer Kraft chassis built by the late Kramer Williamson himself. In Victory Lane, Grasso said, "I'd like to thank Kramer Williamson for building an awesome race car," as emotions poured out from everyone in the winner's circle. The Grasso and Williamson families have grown closer, with Felecia and J.J.'s wife Julie becoming good friends through racing. While family, friends and fans still grieved the loss of Kramer, that night at Selinsgrove Speedway certainly helped the healing process, and everyone who witnessed the events of the night had no doubt Kramer was watching from above with a huge smile on his face.

In the race of life, there are no pit stops, no timeouts, and the race keeps running on and on. In the years after Kramer's passing, there have been many tears, unbelievable stories and heroics shared, tributes, memorials and yes, even healing. The Williamson family continues to go to the races every chance they get. Sharon is always visible and still sells Kramer Williamson T-shirts at various tracks throughout the year, often displaying the #73 Pink Panther. Felecia has a successful life all of her own in the health care industry, continues to live in Pennsylvania, and is right by her mom's side at the races. You can't miss them. They are the two with the biggest smiles and the most pink on at the track, and will talk to anyone who wants to talk about Sprint Car racing. Kurt carries on the Kramer Kraft name and its reputation, building

Kramer takes some warm-up laps on his final night of racing. Kramer left a legacy of kindness and greatness that made everyone who knew him or witnessed him race a better person (by Barry Skelly and Allan Yeager Photography).

high-quality shocks for some of racing's top teams in many of the top series today.

Sportswriter Jeremy Elliott had the best description of Kramer in his later years that I have ever heard. Elliott said, "Williamson was the older brother you wanted to beat because he was that good. He was the loveable uncle, the one who is always cracking people up. And he was the father figure, guiding and teaching young racers." Perhaps everyone loved him so much because that's what we saw in him, too. Whatever the memories people have of Kramer, this much is true: on any weekend around America at a Sprint Car race, someone is telling a story or sharing a memory about the guy who drove a pink Sprint Car, Kramer Williamson. Kramer would always ask his family at the end of a night's racing no matter whether he won or lost, Did we have fun? For the Williamsons, it was always about fun and being with family. For us, the fans, we definitely had fun watching Kramer and we thank him for taking us all along for the ride.

A Thank-You
from the Family

Over Kramer's racing career, there were many people who helped Kramer with sponsorships, spent endless hours working in the shop, and assisted at the track. There were many car owners who helped along the way as well. If I tried to mention everyone's name, I would certainly miss someone and feel terrible. Kramer and I appreciated everything everyone did for us and our race team. I would like to say thank you to everyone, from the bottom of my heart, who helped in any way to make Kramer's career as successful as it was. Also, a big thank-you goes out to the track owners, race teams and fans who have been part of Kramer's life. I say this for Kramer, Kurt, Felecia and myself: THANK YOU ALL!

Sharon Williamson

Bibliography

Books

Hodges, Gerald. *Outlaw Kings*, vol. 1. Daphne, AL: Gerald Hodges Agency, 2014.
Rose, Buzz, and Jim Chini. *The History of the United Racing Club*, vol. 1: *The First Thirty Years, 1948–1977*. Tempe, AZ: Ben Franklin Press, 2007.
_____. *The History of the United Racing Club*, vol. 2: *Tow Money, 1978–2006*. Tempe, AZ: Ben Franklin Press, 2007.

Magazines

Garrepy, Michael. "The Twilight of Kramer Williamson." *Flat Out Illustrated* 1, no. 3 (May–June 2000).
Indiana State Fair Official Program, 1978.
Indiana State Fair Official Program, 1980.
KARS 1976 Yearbook.
KARS 1977 Yearbook.
KARS 1978 Yearbook.
Kreitzer, Al. "Area Auto Racing News." *Silver Spring Speedway 1969 Yearbook*.
_____. "Area Auto Racing News." *Silver Spring Speedway 1971 Yearbook*.
Man and Wheel, 1976.
Penn National Speedway, Official Speedway Program.
Thompson, Bev. "Henry Fenimore Earns First Ever Championship with URC." *URC Yearbook*, 1991.
Unger, Harvey. "Kramer Williamson, A Charger by Choice." *Man and Wheel*, 1977.
_____. "Kramer Williamson, A Man in Control." *Dirt Track Racing Magazine Fall-Winter 1978–79*.
Williams Grove Speedway 1979 National Open Yearbook.
Zimmerman, Cher. "Kramer Williamson, Synonymous with Champion." *URC Yearbook*, 1995.
_____. "A Look at Kramer Williamson." *URC Yearbook*, 1991.
_____. "Vince Gangemi & The Ford, Redemption at Last." *URC Yearbook*, 1995.

Newspapers

Area Auto Racing News: 4/30/1985, 4/16/1985, 5/21/1985, 6/25/1985, 8/31/1985, 6/13/1986, 7/27/1986, 5/7/1991, 6/4/1991.

Daily Item: 8/10/1981.
Evening News: 7/10/1980.
Indianapolis News: 9/6/1980.
National Hawkeye Racing News: 8/15/1985.
Patriot: 8/8/1989.
Sunday Patriot News: 7/6/1980.

Websites

Lehman, Doc. "All Star Super Sprints: The Forgotten Sprint Series." dirt-racers.com. Accessed 2003.

Interviews

Brown, Davey. In-person interview, May 20, 2016.
Cathell, Charlie. Phone interview, August 3, 2016.
Coverdale, Greg. In-person interview, May 19, 2016.
Gustin, Chris. Phone interview, August 8, 2016.
Hamilton, Al. In-person interview, April 30, 2016.
Hamilton, Tim. In-person interview, April 30, 2016.
Hammaker, Dale. In-person interview, April 29, 2016.
Hogue, Tim. In-person interview, April 30, 2016.
Irvin, Cliff. Phone interview, June 16, 2016.
Kreitzer, Al. In-person interview, May 1, 2016.
Paxton, Lynn. In-person interview, May 20, 2016.
Williamson, Felecia. In-person interview, April 29, 2016.
Williamson, George. Phone and in-person interviews, May 2016.
Williamson, Kurtis. Phone interviews, August 2016.
Williamson, Sharon. Phone and in-person interviews, January–August 2016.
Wolfgang, Doug. Phone interview, May 20, 2016.
Zimmerman, John. In-person interview, May 19, 2016.

Index

199